PRAISE FOR STACEY FREEMAN

"Now this is a great read about a very strong woman impacted by divorce who triumphs through adversity and kicks it right between the eyes."

—**Vikki Ziegler**, celebrity divorce attorney, host of Bravo TV's *Untying the Knot*, television personality, and author of *The Premarital Planner: Your Complete Legal Guide to a Perfect Marriage*

"Page-turner. This transformative collection of essays offers thoughtful, relatable insight into Stacey Freeman's personal journey transcending the shame and pain of separation, including surviving transcontinental adultery to arrive at an inner sense of grace and ease. A great read for anyone whose life has been impacted by divorce."

—**Gabrielle Hartley**, divorce attorney and mediator, author *Better Apart: The Radically Positive Way to Separate* and *The Secret to Getting Along: Three Steps to Life-Changing Conflict Resolution*, TEDx speaker

"Stacey Freeman holds nothing back in this unfiltered, unapologetic, and sometimes cringe-worthy account of life through heartbreak and stepping into her fullest self. For anyone who has experienced a grueling breakup, this collection of essays is incredibly relatable and a testament to how empowering our lives can be if we are willing to do the hard (self) work."

—**Erin Levine**, divorce attorney, founder and CEO of Hello Divorce

"Lingerie, bread loaves, and vomit all make an appearance in this engaging compilation of powerful essays on adultery, grief, divorce, single motherhood, online dating, and self-empowerment. Stacey Freeman's writing is riveting and perfectly captures a tapestry of emotions. Her strength of character and fierce dedication to her children will inspire you to be an amazing co-parent."

—**Elise Buie**, divorce attorney, writer, and podcast host

"Stacey Freeman's humor shines through this anthology about picking herself up after betrayal. Instead of being left devastated and bitter, she comes out the other side with a positive attitude and hope for finding love again. Her story demonstrates strength and resilience, making it an important one to share."

—**Cassie Zampa-Keim**, professional matchmaker, founder and CEO of Innovative Match, and author of *Finding Love After 50: Modern Dating Strategies for Women from an Industry Insider*

I Bought My Husband's Mistress Lingerie

Essays by

STACEY FREEMAN

Table of Contents

For Maddy, Lizzy, and Tyler

And anyone who has been hurt by someone they loved. This book is for you.

I Bought My Husband's Mistress Lingerie

January 26, 2012

"Can I help you?" the salesgirl at Victoria's Secret inquired with a smile.

"Yes," I answered, shifting my weight and avoiding her eyes. As I did, I caught my own in a nearby mirror. I barely recognized myself. Then, with sudden resolve, I turned and faced her.

I can do this.

"I'm looking for lingerie," I proclaimed.

My discomfort was obvious. Never before had I bought myself something so . . . lascivious.

As fate would have it, that day would not be an exception.

"Do you have something specific in mind?" the bright-eyed young woman pressed on with overemphasized cheeriness. She must have assumed I was shopping for a romantic night planned for me by my loving husband or doting boyfriend.

I wasn't.

"Yes," I continued with the deliberateness of a woman on a mission. "It's red satin with black lace trim. High above the knee."

"Oh, yes!" she squealed with delight, confident she knew exactly the piece I was referring to.

Was that because she'd recently sold one just like it to another customer before me? As fast as it had entered, I pushed the thought from my mind.

Focus. Just focus.

"It's right over here," the salesgirl pointed, ushering me over to the wall where that now-familiar nightie hung triumphantly in the open. "Would you like to try it on?"

I shook my head. No, that wouldn't be necessary. After all, I wasn't buying it for me. I was buying it for someone else. And I already knew her size.

My husband's open suitcase had sat on the floor of our master bedroom where it always did while he was home, waiting to be unpacked after weeks, sometimes a couple of months, spent away. Business trips, I used to call them. Instead of admitting what they were—a geographical separation—with him working on one side of the world and me living on the other.

A strain on our marriage, no doubt. But when we agreed to this plan, we compared ourselves to military couples who spend long periods away from one another while still remaining committed.

Yet somehow during these "furloughs," my husband's suitcase would never be unpacked. Instead, only its contents rotated, and preparation made for the next business trip. It was a statement—his—that our house was no longer home.

During this last visit, the one that would mark the end of our marriage, I had walked past his open suitcase for days, annoyed as I always was that not only had he failed to unpack it but that he hadn't even moved it into our walk-in closet.

Unlike those other visits, right before this one, my husband announced he was "done with our marriage," leaving me to question whether he had already met someone else. My husband denied any involvement, and I chose to believe him. Never before did I have a reason not to.

But on that particular evening, the appearance of his suitcase struck me as odd. At first, I couldn't quite put my finger on why. It was only when I walked past it for what was probably the hundredth time that week that I stopped dead in my tracks.

My husband was never one for neatness, and I saw what was different; the cover, though left unzipped, was now closed.

I don't know what made me look inside since I never had in the past. But as I lifted the top, I noticed the familiar pink striped bag shoved in between his clothes, inside—you guessed it—a red satin nightie with black lace trim.

Born a fair-skinned strawberry blonde, I was told my entire life how red wasn't my color. As a baby, my mother dressed me almost entirely in pale pinks and soft greens. And for most of my adult life, I abided by that same tradition. The lingerie I held in my trembling hands wasn't for me.

With the vengeance of a woman scorned, I grabbed for my scissors and cut into the fabric, the sound of each breaking thread mimicking the sound of the life I knew being torn to shreds. When I was done, I carefully wrapped the defiled nightie back in its tissue paper, placed it in the bag, and returned the bag to the suitcase, no one ever the wiser. I imagined my husband's mistress opening her gift with excitement, this gesture of romantic love, only to discover it had been destroyed.

The next morning, I confessed my sin.

"You know," my husband advised with the tutelage of a sage, "I'm only going to buy her another one."

And that's when I said it: "I'll do it."

Surely you must be wondering what self-respecting woman would buy her husband's mistress lingerie.

I argue a woman who has self-respect.

For years, I lived with a man who didn't value me. And, for equally as long, I accepted far less—less attention, less respect, and less love—than what I deserved. When I became a scorned wife, I graduated from the class my husband had instructed me in.

Though I've told this story countless times since then, each time I do, I'm met with the same incredulous stares. At first, no one understands. But contrary to popular opinion, my self-respect wasn't lost at Victoria's Secret that morning. In fact, the exact opposite was true.

Within days, I retained an attorney. And, despite my husband and I giving reconciliation a half-hearted shot three months later, I already knew the end had come and welcomed it.

That torn nightie still sits in my lingerie drawer among all the others I bought for myself afterward, a reminder that from ugliness can come beauty and from weakness incredible strength. Not to mention a newfound love for lingerie and the color red.

Do You Believe in Things You Can't Always Understand?

It was ostensibly the least likely place to have one of "those" experiences. You know, the kind that can't be explained. Yet there I was, at the Peninsula Hotel in Beverly Hills, having one.

I was in the early stages of pregnancy, experiencing chronic morning sickness that lasted the entire morning and continued throughout the day into the night. But, uncomfortable as I was, I went ahead anyway and joined my husband on a business trip to LA so that we could spend a relaxing weekend together.

As we sat down at a table in the hotel's bar for a late afternoon bite, I noticed the couple seated next to us. They were hard to miss, looking more interested in tearing each other's clothes off than eating the food in front of them.

My husband and I snickered as we watched these "old" people (in their late forties or early fifties) grope each other, and we whispered that maybe they should go to their room. I wanted to do the same. But what appealed most to me about heading upstairs was the prospect of vomiting in private instead of in the nearby lobby bathroom. Anything apart from that plan remained far from my mind.

So when the inevitable occurred, and I raced toward the nearest restroom, the couple questioned my husband about my hasty exit. Explaining I was pregnant, my husband elaborated that this pregnancy followed a miscarriage the previous year.

Not only was I sick, but I was also anxious this child would meet the same fate.

Once I returned to the table, the woman congratulated me on my pregnancy. She was a sight to see. Tall and statuesque with braids in her hair, she showed just enough of her golden skin, which resembled brown sugar, to look sexy in her blood-orange dress without appearing cheap, despite the plunging v-neckline. Her eyes glistened in the afternoon sunlight that streamed through the windows, and it was hard to avert her stare. As I thanked her, she told me she had been "touched by the hand of God," was clairvoyant, and could help me with my nausea.

"May I?" she asked.

But before I could answer, she began rubbing her hands together. Seconds later, she brought both palms to my face just short of touching it and inched them down my neck and chest until reaching my belly.

I could feel the heat rising from her hands and remember the odd sensation as if it were yesterday. After, she looked at me and said I would have a beautiful and healthy baby girl. She also said I would experience temporary but immediate relief from feeling sick. I welled up with tears at her words while my husband smirked at the woman for her performance and me for believing it.

The couple left. So did my nausea for the rest of the weekend. Then, with each passing hour of relief, I became more panicked that my pregnancy was in trouble, nausea being my only proof this alien-like being inside me was alive and well.

Later that summer, my husband and I welcomed a healthy baby girl as predicted and, fourteen months later, a second daughter. Three and a half years after that, our son was born. As I look back, each pregnancy had been more mellow than the one before it.

Naysayers will argue my miraculous "cure" resulted purely from the power of suggestion. I beg to differ. I felt something different that afternoon, something ethereal, and I like to think it was more than this stranger's reassurances because failing to do so would mean we're not part of something larger than our own existence.

I believe we are.

That said, I believe in free will. I believe we each have a choice as to whether we feel good and, in the same vein, whether we're happy. Yes, you read that correctly. We must want these things for ourselves. And though we may say we do, failing to take affirmative steps to create happiness can mean the difference between living a full and peaceful existence and meandering through a life of sadness, regret, or indifference.

Author J.K. Rowling once said, "[r]ock bottom became the solid foundation on which I rebuilt my life." On some days, I can argue I hit rock bottom when my marriage ended—when I discovered my husband was leaving me and for another woman no less. I might tell you on other days it was when I learned my father had died. And on still others, that it was when I miscarried my first pregnancy.

Rock bottom is not easy to discern. There's no way to know when we've hit it until we've gotten up and something else has come along to challenge us. And no matter how hard we try to predict what's around the bend, even to the extent of visiting psychics (which I've done over the years), we can't. However, if there's one thing I know for sure, it's that we can affect our destiny.

Have I hit rock bottom? Maybe. Knowing how fragile and unpredictable life is, I certainly hope so. But I also suspect I haven't. Yet I refuse to sit here and wait for the other shoe to drop, even if I do sometimes fall victim to the "why's": why is this happening to me, or why is this my life? To date, such questions remain rhetorical, though I know the answers will be revealed in due time.

So yes, I do believe in those things I can't always understand, if only for the reason that we each have the wherewithal to ascribe meaning to our lives. The lessons are there. But we must choose to learn them.

Lusting for Love

Until age thirty-nine, I had sex with only one man, my husband. We met in high school and fell in love. However, my first sexual experience was far from romantic. We were fooling around on my bedroom floor, and it kind of just . . . happened.

I cried in the bathroom, staring down at my blood-stained underpants, thinking, "What have I done?"

Not long afterward, I experienced spotting between my periods, and my mother took me to her gynecologist. The doctor, who was in his forties, had a daughter my age. He appeared to be just another dad.

I don't know of any woman who enjoys a trip to the gynecologist or any girl who isn't nervous about her first. The sterility of the room, the uncomfortable table, the stirrups, the speculum; it was all so antiseptic, and as a teenager, I was petrified.

The doctor advised my mother and me beforehand how he would prescribe birth control pills only if I were sexually active as my periods would likely regulate naturally. When my mother left, the doctor asked if I had already had sex, reminding me anything I said would be confidential. I told him yes.

As he inserted the speculum, I squirmed in discomfort and told him I was afraid. Instead of reassuring me, he was abrupt: "I don't have time for this." Then he stormed out of the room. There I sat—alone, cold, fragile—in that paper gown that adds to feeling so vulnerable. When the doctor returned, I composed myself and stared straight up at the ceiling as he examined me roughly.

When he finished, he asked, "Do you climax?

I was frozen, unsure what to say.

"Excuse me?" I whispered, not because I didn't understand the question but because I couldn't believe he had asked it.

He repeated himself: "Do. You. Climax."

"Excuse me?" I managed to croak a little louder this time.

"I just want to know if the sex is worth it," was his response.

Stunned, I remained silent as I watched him walk out, letting the door slam behind him.

I dressed quickly, leaving that office and hoping never to return. In the hallway, my mother emerged from another room with tears streaming down her cheeks. The doctor had told her. Disappointment was written all over her face.

Back at home, my mother was still crying, as was I. She scolded me for having sex and ordered me to stop. It was a de facto cease and desist order. I felt cheap, like I was one of "those" girls, even though I wasn't. My mother was a single parent and presumably felt she needed additional support. She rushed to fill in my grandparents, her best friend, even the cleaning lady.

I was humiliated.

My boyfriend and I continued to date (and have sex) until we married when I was twenty-two. Our sex life was the only one I knew. It was safe and comfortable and, as the years passed, boring. It was rare that I craved sex and could go months without it. I loved my husband but was no longer in love with him or attracted to him.

So when I found myself suddenly separated at thirty-nine, I was still sexually inexperienced, despite a twenty-four-year relationship that included sixteen years of marriage and three children.

My next first occurred when I met a man online and went out on my second first date as a newly single woman. He was my polar opposite as far as sexual experience goes. Never married at forty-six, he had nearly thirty years of experience under his belt. Although highly educated and clean-cut, he oozed sexuality in a way that only a bad boy could. The first time we had sex was a rite of passage into womanhood. It wasn't romantic; it was thrilling.

This man represented everything that married life was not. He lived alone in a Manhattan apartment equipped with a flat-screen TV, a bedroom without a lamp, a bed without a headboard, and a nightstand filled with condoms. He was charismatic and could make me melt with the flash of a smile. At first, I thought he was elusive, but, in reality, he was emotionally unavailable, making it impossible to get to know him.

On and off over the next twenty months, he became the college fling I never had. The problem was college flings are meant to come and go, and this one lasted well past its expiration date. He finally kicked my ass to the curb when he announced he had met someone only days after we were last together.

Since the day I laid eyes on him, I lusted for this man. But he never wanted an exclusive relationship with me, so, as time

21

wore on, I came away feeling sad and empty after our visits. What I truly lusted for was love and intimacy. Naively, I hung on to the hope of that happening, which it never did.

His purpose in my life is now clear: he drew me away from the man I loved and toward the woman I was growing into, a woman who is confident and comfortable with her sexual identity.

The irony is, even today, whenever I have sex with a new partner, and there have been few to date, I inevitably revert to my teenage self, feeling a slight tinge of shame for my transgression. I imagine it is because I have yet to find the right man. I know when I do, and there is that perfect combination of love and lust, I will feel no shame at all. Only joy.

On the Courthouse Steps: The Day I Settled with Myself

I spent more than a year planning my wedding. Sixteen years of marriage (twenty-four together), three children, two apartments (on two separate continents), two houses, two cats, and one dog later, I spent nearly the same amount of time planning my divorce. But no amount of planning could have prepared me for that isolated moment when I officially became single again.

Planning a wedding in my early twenties with the only man I ever dated, and straight from my mother's home, my future unfolding before me like some capricious, unscripted romance novel, I felt as though I had the world in the palm of my hand. With promising legal careers for both of us (though mine never happened), the expectation of a happy home filled with laughing children (dream fulfilled, at least for a while), and boundless opportunity for travel, culture, and affluence (check, check, check), my early concept of marriage did not extend far beyond those superficial wedding day plans for music, flowers, and menu selections designed to perfect the celebration that would send us down our golden path in ignorance.

As time wore on, and the picture-perfect life I had once envisioned faded until it finally became singed with years of disappointment, heartache, and eventually my husband's unfaithfulness as his chosen career path directed him to live in Hong Kong apart from our children and me, a job prospect about which he and I disagreed, I found myself standing on the courthouse steps about to become a forty-year-old divorcée.

I spent more than a year planning for that day, my divorce day, attending countless meetings with lawyers, forensic accountants, financial planners, marriage counselors, and therapists. But really, nothing could have prepared me for that morning, that single moment, when the first chapters of my life would finally come to a close.

As I stood in the courtroom before a judge, answering rote queries from my lawyer, those silly factual inquiries whose answers were already known but were still required to extricate me from my marriage (On what date were you married? How many children do you have together?), my husband listening via conference call from his comfortable new home in his comfortable new life 8,000 miles away, I felt an overwhelming sense of foreboding. There I was, now middle-aged, about to be thrust alone into the world for, in essence, the first time in my life. With each stabbing question, my uncertain future drew closer until I officially, however begrudging I was, was forced to accept and settle for my new title—divorced.

Unlike my wedding, there was no fanfare following my divorce. No music. No celebration. Only quiet. A friend who divorced weeks earlier had just recalled to me how her ex-husband called minutes after their proceeding ended. Like mine, it took place via conference call with a husband who had likewise relocated to Asia without her. As I exited the courthouse, a part of me secretly hoped I would receive such a call. But my cell phone never rang. There was no heartfelt goodbye. No apologies exchanged. No nod to the years we spent together. No closure, only the deafening silence of our broken promises.

I never did receive that call, though today, I no longer wait for it.

The months since have been bittersweet. With each passing day, as I picked my children and myself up and began writing the next chapters of my story, I realized my title of divorcée is not to be shied away from, but, rather, embraced. Where I once thought of my marriage as early chapters of a tragic love story, I now say those pages told the tale of a romance that ran its course. Today, I am writing the paragraphs not of a new chapter but an entirely new book.

A friend recently told me that I have never looked better. When she said it, I was incredulous. After all, she first met me when I was in my early thirties, not long after the birth of my third child, and arguably when my marriage was good. Eight years older, I thought there was no possible way I could look better than I did back then.

When I came home and looked in the mirror that evening, I realized she was right. But it was not because of a new hairstyle or the shedding of past baby weight. It was because today I have made peace with myself, settling the unease I once felt with a title I neither asked for nor expected. For the first time in my life, I actually respected the woman I saw looking back at me.

And it was not in spite of her divorce. It was because of it.

Visiting Tulum: Revisiting the Past and Reinventing the Future

I spent this past Christmas break on a ten-day vacation with my three children. They were not supposed to be with me, so when I learned we would be together over the holidays, I scrambled to find us a last-minute solution for spending quality time together as a family away from home. This was to be our first real family vacation alone with no grandparents along for the ride and certainly no husband to assume part of the responsibility.

Three nights in Houston followed by a seven-day cruise to Costa Maya, Belize, and Cozumel. Not quite roughing it, but a significant undertaking for any single parent nonetheless.

The children's behavior during this trip was, to say the least, less than stellar. There were fights over card games, who said what to whom, who looked at each other the wrong way, and who touched whose body. Complaints were likewise the order of the day, every day. The boat was too rocky and the beds too hard. You name it; they fought or complained about it. My patience was tested in a biblical sense. At the time, I could not understand their angst and lamented daily that, for this aggravation, I could have stayed home for free.

On day five of the cruise, our ship docked in Cozumel, Mexico, for a pre-arranged shore excursion to visit the Maya ruins in Tulum. We left our cabin at six o'clock in the morning to eat a big breakfast in anticipation of sightseeing all day, amid even more fighting and complaints.

I had visited Tulum with my ex-husband back in 1997, early on in our marriage, before our first child was born. I knew it would be a learning experience for the children considering their respective school curriculums. But I could never have imagined the life lessons we all would ultimately take away from that day.

While I stood there staring at the ruins more than sixteen years later, without my husband but with our three children by my side, my feelings were bittersweet. Like .the civilization the Maya worked so hard to build, now evidenced only by the rubble lying around us, the marriage my husband and I spent sixteen years building lay in a similar state of disrepair. But, as our tour guide educated us, the legacy of the Maya continues to live on in present-day Mexican culture, as I recognized does the legacy my ex-husband and I started to build lives on in the three children we created together.

That night before bed, my eight-year-old son broke down crying: "I miss Daddy. He should be here with us. I hate her. I wish she would just go away, and then he could come back."

Of course my son was talking about my ex-husband's significant other, whom he was "seeing" while we were still married. It did not take long for my two daughters to join in, shedding tears along with their brother. Watching all the families together at holiday time had been weighing on them throughout the week, which I am pretty sure was the reason for their bad behavior.

I was shocked. It had already been a while since my ex-husband and I decided to separate. Were these children actually still holding out hope their father and I would someday reconcile? I certainly was not, so how could they?

To three wide-eyed children, I explained yet again that Daddy is not coming back to me, no matter what becomes of his relationship with someone else. Whether or not it fully sank in, I am still skeptical. What I did emphasize to my children, and I hope to have illustrated to them during our trip, is that although their father is not a part of their day-to-day lives, there are still good times to be had with each of their parents individually and new memories to be made. Although no longer a couple, we are still their family and will forever share the privilege of being their parents.

The Maya believed they could use their calendar to predict the future. Although their prophecy for the end of the world did not, thankfully, come to fruition, they did serve to illustrate that legacies continue for years and years to come.

Civilizations change, and so do families. But life goes on, just in a different form.

My New Year's Eve Kiss

I've never loved the fanfare of New Year's Eve. For many, it's a time to dress up and be grand. But for me, New Year's Eve has, over time, become a night for quiet reflection, a night to appreciate the subtleties and nuances in my life that have brought me to this day another year later.

At one extreme, New Year's Eve has signaled monumental changes in my life. It was on this night back in 1987 when I went on my first date with the seventeen-year-old high school boy who, eight years later, would become my husband. It was also a New Year's Eve that would become the last night we would spend together as husband and wife following a twenty-four-year relationship together.

New Year's Eve was the day back in 2002 when my husband and I watched the ball drop in Hong Kong, both of us bleary-eyed as our two and three-year-old daughters played with their toys at our feet. They were jet-lagged and confused that night was now day while we contemplated, with what felt like the weight of the world on our shoulders, whether we should move there. It was this night that directed the course of our marriage, setting it on a path toward its eventual dissolution.

At the other extreme, New Year's Eve was another time when I stayed up all night sick with a stomach virus. Or a night of dancing and fun as my husband and I celebrated my college friend's wedding just four months after our own. Or the night we hosted a dinner party for close family and friends in our new home.

Still, it was always the simplest moments in life that created my most vivid memories. I remember well the cloth calendar that hung in our kitchen when I was a little girl. My mother bought the same one each year at a local stationery store, and together, my mother, brother, and I would pick out a new pattern every December.

Whenever my mother brought the calendar home, she hung the new one behind the old one. And every year, just after midnight, my younger brother would run to the kitchen and take the now out-of-date calendar down to reveal its replacement behind it. Always flashing a bright smile from ear to ear, always hopeful the coming year would be better than the one before it.

When my father passed away following a massive heart attack in December of 1985, the month became a blur. Hanukkah came and went without notice as we sat Shiva through most of the holiday. When the Shiva visits ended, and the platters of food stopped arriving, the silence in my house became deafening and my outlook dismal.

We spent that New Year's Eve at home, the three of us watching the ball drop with Dick Clark on TV. The weather was cold and unwelcoming, and our house no longer felt like a home. At thirteen, I couldn't imagine I would ever have anything else to look forward to.

As the clock struck midnight, my mother turned to kiss each of us. But my brother wasn't there. We called out to him throughout the house and finally found him in the kitchen, standing beside where the calendars hung with the old one in his hands and a grin on his face. It was, after all, a new year, and my ten-year-old brother still recognized enough hope around him to look forward to the future in spite of how hopeless things were that day.

Last New Year's Eve was my first without my husband. I chose to spend the night in my mother's home, back in my old teenage bedroom, forgoing the opportunity to spend the evening with a guy I knew wasn't right for me or me for him. Doing so meant it would be the first New Year's Eve in twenty-five years without anyone to kiss me at midnight.

This year, I'm enjoying a quiet New Year's Eve at home with my mother, stepfather, and three children. I'm lucky to be surrounded by people I love who love and support me. That said, not having a significant other is disappointing. And maybe that makes me selfish because I already have so much in my life yet still want more. But I can't help it. I believe the right person is out there for me.

So tonight, in my mind's eye, I will change that old kitchen calendar as my brother did years ago and welcome in a new year, one filled with appreciation for the blessings I have and hope for the New Year's Eve kiss I do not.

Parenting after Divorce: Why I Won't Double Down This Valentine's Day

My children love Valentine's Day. After all, what's not to love? For them, Valentine's Day means funny greeting cards, pretty red heart-shaped boxes filled with chocolates, fuzzy themed pajama pants, and stuffed animals. However, more recently, it has come to mean something different for me.

After separating, my ex-husband and I each assumed our own gift-giving responsibilities and, without thinking, doubled down on gifts by celebrating every holiday twice. In an era already marred by excessive materialism, my children now, knowingly and happily, receive double what they had before. As I watched them become adept players in a high-stakes game, one where their values were at stake, I decided that this Valentine's Day, all bets are off.

Listening to them speculate on what each of their parents will give them this Valentine's Day has been turning my stomach for days. So at lunchtime, I gave the three of them an assignment: come up with a list of five things they love about each of their siblings or activities they love to do with each other. I told them I would do the same for them. Our lists, which must be created with thought, will be read aloud at a family dinner I am organizing this Friday night to celebrate the holiday.

As I made my announcement, I was greeted with eye rolls from my twelve and thirteen-year-old daughters. My eight-year-old son, however, was on board. The winter has been hard, with too many snow days spent cooped up in the house. It is safe to say that we have all been getting on each other's nerves. I think my son was grateful for an opportunity to sway the mood.

After lunch, to my surprise, the children began working hard on their respective lists. When they finished, they brought their musings to me one by one, so I would know they took the project seriously.

As I read what they love about each other, I noticed that not one entry had anything to do with material possessions. "I love your beautiful curly hair," one child wrote. "Your strength is something I love," another listed. "I love how every time we fight, we always make up and become the closest sisters in the world again," wrote the last child.

I was more than pleasantly surprised. One of my children wrote her list as an acrostic poem, using the first letters of her siblings' names to begin every line. Another child added photos to her lists, personalizing them even further. Regardless of format, every list was created with kindness and respect. I was moved.

We never ended up getting out of the house today. The weather outside was cold, and, as usual, it started to snow. But for the remainder of the afternoon and evening, the children enjoyed each other's company without fighting. They played cards and board games, watched movies, and talked. It was an ordinary day that turned out to be most memorable.

On Friday, we will celebrate Valentine's Day together as a family. I already announced that I would buy each of them something small to acknowledge the holiday. Gifts will not be the focus. To my delight, no one complained.

My middle child did express concern that there is no special man in my life who will give me something for Valentine's Day. At that, I simply smiled. My daughter didn't realize how she and her siblings had already given me a far greater gift than I could ever have hoped for.

My Field of Dreams: If I Build It, Happiness Will Come

> "The one constant through all the years . . . has been baseball. America has rolled by like an army of steamrollers. It has been erased like a blackboard, rebuilt, and erased again. But baseball has marked the time. This field, this game: it's a part of [the] past . . . It reminds us of all that once was good and that could be again." —Terence Mann, *Field of Dreams, 1989*

I don't know a lot about baseball. But I do love the game. I also have a deep-seated hatred for it.

My father loved the Yankees. I remember him lying on my parents' bed, leaning on one arm, watching the games with quiet delight, at peace, if only for a moment. He took me to my first baseball game at Yankee Stadium when I was around eleven. I still remember the awe I felt as I contemplated the field's grandness for the first time. It was larger than life, and I felt tiny. But like any piece of a jigsaw puzzle, I knew even then that somehow I belonged to baseball and baseball to me.

My brother began playing tee-ball when he was five. That spring, and every spring after, my father would toss a baseball with my brother on our front lawn. A neighbor with her toddler daughter in a stroller would often wave as they passed our house on their daily walks.

Every spring when a new Little League season began, my father would come to the games, cheering from the bleachers. He watched with pride as his son played, the son named after his father, my grandfather, who died years before his time.

When my brother was ten, my father died, and my brother's fan club lost a member. Attending Little League games with only my mother transformed those unremarkable occasions of which happy childhoods are made into remembrances of profound sadness.

Every other kid on the team had their dad there to cheer for him, to run onto the field, to help with his swing, to go out for ice cream afterward, and to celebrate a big win. That same spring, our little neighbor, while out for one of her walks, passed by our house. As her mother told it, seeing the empty driveway, she questioned who would now play catch with my brother. It was after that season my brother stopped playing baseball. Baseball had been stilled, if not stolen, from my childhood, and I was glad to see it gone. The pain of its altered state was unbearable.

Baseball re-entered my life when I returned to Yankee Stadium as a teen. Like my father, my ex-husband is a Yankee fan, and it was he who reacquainted me with the familiar and comforting sounds of the game. Over the next twenty-four years, we attended games, first as a couple, then as a family. Following our separation, my ex-husband began taking the children without me. I was no longer invited, now a mere spectator to my former life. Baseball was, again, quieted from my world.

When my son turned eight, he began playing Little League like his father and grandfather before him. Doing so is a notable rite of passage for any kid and a milestone worthy of celebration. Yet, there I found myself again, sitting at a game watching a young, innocent boy play baseball without his father to cheer him on. Though this time, not because of death but because of divorce. A consequence of choice, not fate.

It was during this season, the season of my divorce, that I failed my son.

Because my children's father lives and works 8,000 miles away and, as a consequence, attended only one of his games, I felt the pressure of single parenting more than ever. I was overwhelmed, sad, and unable to focus. Yes, I was there physically as I sat behind third base. But I didn't cheer. I stared straight at the games but didn't watch. My thoughts were elsewhere, anywhere else than on the reality that there I was, alone, no husband, no father for my children to share in their day-to-day lives. My family seemed beyond repair.

But as my son's team started to win game after game, my eyes began to flutter, and I was lured from my haze. The championship game was a nail-biter, a scene straight out of a feel-good movie. There stood all the parents on pins and needles, hands clutched to the chain-link fence in anticipation, cheering on the team. Parents exchanged hugs and words of congratulations with one another as every child contributed in his or her own right to the win, which eventually came on that beautiful sunny morning.

It was on that day I won too. Although I wasn't yet aware, it was to become the day when I would reclaim my family, my team, now with me as its head coach.

After the game, my son stood with his team for pictures and collected his yearbook. But I was disturbed at how unexcited and withdrawn he looked. This was not a child whose team had just won a championship game. Family Day was to follow, a celebration for every team in the league. But my son wanted to go home and pleaded more and more with me to leave every time I urged him to stay.

As we headed to the parking lot, endless happy families walking toward us, I once again felt defeated by divorce. But I knew that letting my son dictate the course of the day could impact the course of his life. This was a day to be remembered, savored, a day to be recognized for hard work, achievement, and camaraderie, not a day to wallow alone in self-pity. So with one quick call to a friend, she and I coaxed my son back to the field, where he spent the afternoon eating and socializing with neighbors and friends, young and old. It was on this day that I showed him baseball isn't just a game. It's happiness. It's family. It's home.

Baseball season will once again be upon us. The past year has been long, and I've been working hard at building my life anew. In so many ways, I know that my children's perceptions turn on my own. But I'm confident that as I find my happiness, so will they. Today, I'm proud to say that my head is back in the game.

Baseball has marked the innings of my life. But it's not the bottom of the ninth just yet. And this team still has a lot more playing to do.

Field Trips, Frights, and Forgiveness

I hate field trips.

There. I confess. I have three children, the oldest of whom is thirteen, and I am ~~embarrassed~~ proud to say the last time I went on a class trip while any of my kids were in elementary school was, um, never.

Go ahead and gasp. Judge me. I. Don't. Care.

I have been a class mother for each kid, one more than once (for the child my two daughters claim is the favorite but who shall remain nameless). I was a Brownies troop leader (and, no, we didn't camp out at Bloomingdale's), I chaired the Girl Scouts Sweetheart Dance (I was kind of inducted against my will into that one, but I still count it anyway), and I have volunteered at countless other school events.

It has always been my pleasure to help. OK, OK, most of the time, that is.

Yet, somehow, the thought of being trapped on a school bus with dozens of kids and no way to escape has always freaked me out. (Actually, in our school district, it was an air-conditioned charter bus with television screens to play movies, but that's beside the point.) However, Friday afternoon, because of my son's seasonal asthma, I had to suck it up (no pun intended) and attend, inhaler in hand.

At 9:00 a.m., I boarded the bus for the hour-long trip each way to what, in my mind, is one of the ickiest and most frightening places on Earth—a bugseum. That's right. An entire museum devoted to those tiny creatures I hate and fear most—bugs.

As the morning progressed, we learned all about millipedes, cockroaches, and, the scariest, tarantulas. (I politely declined my opportunity to pet one, thank you very much.) But I was happy to be there, given how I began witnessing my son getting sicker by the minute starting mid-morning.

By the time lunch was done, he had opted to sit with me on the bus for the return ride home, no longer caring if he didn't look cool sitting with his mom. I knew he wasn't feeling well because this was the same kid who warned me before getting out of the car for school that morning that I should socialize with the other moms on the trip, stay off my iPad, and not use foul language. (I think I permanently scarred the kid when not that long ago I fell into a snow embankment on the walk from school to my car and yelled "Shit!" as I landed flat on my ass in front of some of his classmates.)

I never claimed to be June fucking Cleaver.

When we got home that afternoon, I sat my son on the couch with a cup of tea and gave him his allergy medication. And after an early dinner at home, we wound up in the hospital emergency room, the field trip no mother ever wants to chaperone.

As I looked around the ER while my son endured three uncomfortable rounds on the nebulizer, I recalled all the other times I waited with my children in the ER, without my husband, for various reasons—fractures, sprains, high fevers, and stomach pains. I began to feel that familiar tinge of rage, irritation, and sadness over my need to always go it alone, even during the days when I was married.

But that night, I stopped myself cold.

Listening to your child struggle to catch his breath is one of the scariest and worst sounds in the world. How I must have sounded to others after all these months as I vented each time I got angry or was disappointed in my ex's behavior, behavior I am powerless to control or change. So instead, I caught my own breath and stayed silent. When my son asked for his dad, I dialed the phone, handed it to him, and continued reading my book without another word or thought.

After being discharged, we returned home, my son breathing with ease. And for the first time since I could remember, I was too.

Today I Accomplished Nothing, and I'm OK With That

When I was growing up, Margaret Mitchell's *Gone with the Wind* was one of my favorite books. I read it as a teenager and later saw the movie. I always envied Scarlett O'Hara, the female heroine, for her ability to emerge steadfast and strong as her world was turned upside down.

So last night, I made a mental list of the tedious yet necessary chores I needed to do today during the six-and-a-half-hour school day. Among them were balancing my checkbook, paying bills, making overdue phone calls, folding laundry, and going to the supermarket. And how many of those tasks did I complete? Absolutely none.

Since I became a mother more than thirteen years ago, I haven't worked outside the home. My home and family became my career, and I managed my life as if it were a corporation. My checkbook was balanced daily (to the penny), every bill was paid on time, the laundry hampers were always empty, and the inside of every closet could compete with a Gap ad. Dinners were homemade and delicious, and my kids were poster children for little suburbanite overachievers. It was all picturesque and perfect.

But not really.

One day, poof, my marriage blew up in smoke. With one sentence from my husband, my life of bullshit came to a screeching halt.

But the thing is, I still had to get out of bed in the morning. No matter how crappy I felt. I had to prepare breakfast for my kids, pack school lunches, wash clothes, make beds, buy food, and cook dinner. I didn't have the luxury of curling up in a ball and dying. I had responsibilities, and I needed to keep going, if not for myself, for them. As the only parent in residence, raising them was—and is—on me.

Not that it wasn't on me before. It was. But when I got separated, it was different. My workaholic husband had left our home for good, so there was no longer another body to pick up even the littlest bit of slack. If I couldn't drive through the carpool line because I was heaving over the toilet with a stomach virus, then no one was going to school.

Throughout each day of my old life, I would have little competitions with myself to see how many chores I could stuff into one day. On a typical day, I woke up at 5:30 a.m. and packed three lunches, made a breakfast for my kids that could rival one at the Four Seasons, arrived extra early in the carpool line at dismissal time so rain would never touch my children's delicate heads for fear they might melt, and prepared traditional meals at dinnertime. And if, God forbid, someone didn't like what was on the menu, well, I whipped up a comparable substitute.

I was woman. Could you hear me roar?

This is no longer my reality. Not because I can't make it so but because I no longer want to.

Don't get me wrong. My house is tidy, the beds are made, and the children are clean and well-fed. The thing is now, on some nights, I may order in Chinese food for dinner. And there may be an occasional day, like yesterday's snow day, when I don't make the beds. And guess what. The sky didn't fall down because there were unmade beds!

My divorce forced me to take stock. Everything around me was pretty, pristine, and perfect, yet my life was anything but that. I was in a loveless marriage, filled with constant arguing and profound loneliness.

Now divorced, I am no longer compensating for what I was lacking.

Today, I revel in the fact there is sometimes an unopened pile of mail, laundry to be folded, or dishes to be washed. I am not going to take care of those things in lieu of living my life to its fullest. These days, I make time to care for my family and myself. I focus on my children's futures and my own, a future with, hopefully, a burgeoning new career that I love.

My children and I ate an early dinner together, a dinner I cooked. But in a couple of hours, I am going to a fundraising event with a friend. Yes, there are still dishes in the sink, and, no, the laundry still isn't folded. But who really cares anyway?

As Scarlett O'Hara said, "I'll think about that tomorrow."

Celebrating Birthdays Post-Divorce: Putting the Happy Back in Birthday

"Happy birthday, sweet boy."

I whispered these words in my son's ear as I gave him soft kisses on his still baby-like cheek to wake him up this morning, the morning of his ninth birthday. It was a perfect scene.

In my mind.

In reality, my voice cracked as I over-enunciated each syllable while yelling the words from my bedroom down the hall, next ordering him into the shower without passing Go. I then scrambled to get dressed so I could start (and finish) all the birthday party preparation I used to do weeks in advance, now two hours before the party.

Birthday parties used to be my forte, my pièce de résistance. As a mother of three, I've probably planned well over forty birthday parties since my first child was born. Invitations were always sent weeks in advance with the etiquette expected of a wedding or other comparable formal event. Favors were personalized and thought out. Party rooms were decorated by theme and filled with colorful balloons and an overabundance of treats.

Not this year.

Since my separation, my ability to focus on small details, those elements one might describe with condescension as minutiae, has sharply waned. Whereas my former self reveled in the opportunity to throw parties and flaunt my skills as the quintessential stay-at-home mom, my current self no longer has the enthusiasm necessary to go to these lengths. In fact, I don't even try.

An onlooker might argue my newfound apathy implies depression and the harsh truth that I no longer take satisfaction in buying color-coordinated paper plates, napkins, and cups as a sign of my despair. I won't lie. A dark cloud hovers above our house. Going through a divorce that results in your ex becoming a physically absent father can do that.

But I'm not sad. Not anymore. I'm happy. Purposefully so. I must be, for the sake of my children. Make no mistake, though; I'm not a hero. I'm simply a mother who loves her kids.

As parents, we know there's no worse pain than watching our children suffer. For a week, my son complained and cried that his father wouldn't be here on his birthday. Again. While I'm helpless to change that particular outcome, I'm not powerless. Through example, I can lead. No matter how difficult, I strive to remain positive even when negative thoughts fight to bring me down.

I no longer obsess over details, which I now see as distractions. I'm only interested in overall perceptions, specifically how we survey our existing landscape and project what lies beyond the horizon.

This afternoon, fifteen third-graders, all school friends, played baseball together at an indoor sports facility. Together they ran, batted, and fielded. They laughed and spent time celebrating their friend—my son. And with good reason, too, because his birthday, his young life with all of its innocence and future promise, is an unequivocal reason to celebrate.

No, my son's father wasn't there to hold the video camera, sing "Happy Birthday," and support him as he used to. But for an hour and a half, my son had fun and forgot his disappointment. For a fleeting moment, all was right with the world.

So when I served the pizza and realized I forgot to bring napkins, I shrugged it off. I didn't chastise myself. I didn't turn a small mistake into a symbol of all my failings and those I absorb on behalf of others.

Too many days have already been stained by sadness because of my divorce, circumstances well beyond any child's control. As a single mom, I understand the onus is on me to make sure my son's special day, and every other day, is memorable, even in its apparent ordinariness, in its potential to be forgotten, at least for the time being.

Today, along with good friends and close family, I, or rather we, helped to do just that. No day is perfect, but this one came pretty close simply because it wasn't.

Why Since Separating I No Longer View My Kids' Camp Photos Online

I confess: It's mid-July, and although my three kids are spread out all over the country at sleepaway camp and on teen tours, I've yet to log in to search for their pictures online. That's right, not once. Gasp if you want, clutch your chest in horror (What a shanda!), and shake your head in dismay. I understand your initial reaction. Not so long ago, it would've been my own.

I get you're angry. Even worried. After all, I've shirked my responsibility as an overbearing Jewish mother, bucked the system, and must, as if by explanation for my slight to overindulgent moms everywhere, be suffering from depression or experiencing a breakdown.

Sorry to disappoint. My choice is deliberate. I'm one hundred percent lucid.

I don't deny it. I wasn't always like this. The summer my two girls went off to sleepaway camp in 2009, I waited at the computer with bated breath for photos of my children to be posted. I was the animated mom in that YouTube video circulating a few summers ago. You know, the one poking fun at mothers who sit hunched over their computers hitting refresh, refresh, refresh until new pictures of their kids relishing in summer fun away from their well-to-do homes magically appear.

I, too, scoured each online photo with fine precision, with skill comparable to a detective's, looking for proof—any hint of a smile, any glimpse of my gifted progeny in the background of some other kid's photo, even a lone body part in a crowd to indicate my child, like all the others, was elated. If that wasn't enough, I saved every (and I mean every) photo in a computer file, even the *Where's Waldo?* ones, to create a professional-looking personalized camp yearbook for my children replete with fancy layouts, witty captions, and heartfelt quotes borrowed from camp newsletters. Such a project took me months to complete, and I presented my labor of love during every Hanukkah to come until the year my husband walked out.

The summer following my separation was emotionally grueling. It was also the summer I stopped looking at camp pictures online. I just couldn't anymore. I needed my days to mourn the end of my marriage and learn how to self-soothe. Friends would approach me and remark how happy my kids looked at camp. I would smile politely, pretending I knew the photos of which they spoke, pretending to know how happy their children were, too, always grateful to receive such positive reviews but never missing the approval if I didn't get it.

One friend, eventually realizing my secret, took it upon herself to save pictures of my eldest daughter as she scanned for her own and emailed them to me regularly while remarking ever so subtly that she knew I didn't look. I did look at the ones she sent and saved the so-called happy evidence on my computer, even using some of them in the montage for my girls' b'not mitzvah celebration. No one was ever the wiser. But I never asked for this service, not ever, and I would've been equally content without it.

Though the wounds from my failed marriage have begun to heal, I've stuck to my new habit, or non-habit, I should say, of not viewing my kids' summer photos online. I don't feel the need, and I'm definitely lighter without the added pressure of keeping up with the daily, even hourly, addition of photos to the camp's website.

Instead, I talk and text with my daughters regularly (teen tours allow unlimited phone privileges), and I email my son, who's spending seven weeks at sleepaway camp, almost every night. Notice I said almost. Yes, I admit there have been nights when I didn't email (please hold your condemnation until I finish), like the days he and I spoke on the phone as well as a couple of other nights when I was out late, and it slipped my mind.

But I didn't berate myself about it afterward as I would've in the past. Why? Because I was confident someone else my son loves and who loves him—his dad, sisters, or grandparents— sent him an email that same day or mailed a letter that week and he would receive some piece of correspondence from someone somewhere despite my forgetfulness. And if by chance he didn't, if it just so happened he failed to hear from anyone back home for an entire twenty-four hours, so be it. I'm that confident my son knows I love him. I continue to demonstrate my love as I always have. It's just that looking at camp pictures no longer constitutes one of the ways I do.

Don't misunderstand. It's not that I'm uninterested or don't care. I'm over the moon that my children are enjoying the summer that my ex-husband and I planned and financed for them. I'm thrilled my children have the privilege of spending their summer with old friends and new ones, participating in activities and sports they enjoy, and, in my daughters' cases, traveling to some of the most picturesque national parks and monuments in the western United States.

But now that I've ushered in a new life—one filled with varying interests, deep passions, and defined goals—I look forward to viewing the personal photos my girls shot of their summer adventures after they return home. I look forward to being an attentive and enthusiastic listener as each of my children recalls stories of their summers away. I look forward to savoring how they're growing into smart, independent, and interesting people I love, respect, and whose company I enjoy—with some moderation.

I no longer sit by idly waiting and watching to see how someone else, even my own children, lives their life. I no longer take full responsibility for anyone else's happiness or sole blame for anyone's lack of it, only for my own. I do my best. Always. I mother my children. I worry about them. I provide for their needs. I nurture them. I love them. But what I no longer do is live vicariously through them.

For me, that's the most refreshing picture of all.

Stay-at-Home Mom Shaming: Move Over Slut Shaming. You Have Company.

"What do you do all day?"

It is an age-old question. Also, it is a frustrating one. However, today it is not being asked by whom you would expect. That is, by the Ward Cleaver-like guy who works all day and expects his hot dinner on the table by six and his hot wife in the bedroom by nine.

Rather, it is a question being asked by women, especially by those who work outside the home, to other women. Asked by those who claim to do and have it all, immediately shaming the stay-at-home mom into justifying how she spends her day. But the real question is: is today's modern woman justified in asking?

Whether a woman is raising one, two, or nineteen children, she is not immune to scrutiny. In an era where more and more women bring home the bacon, fry it up in a pan, attend four travel soccer games and three birthday parties, drop off and pick up from two soccer practices, and serve as a judge for a high school forensics tournament all in a single weekend, the woman who does not fall into one of the #girlsruntheworld categories—doctor, lawyer, executive—is put on the defensive.

She is told, though usually not directly, that she does not measure up. Cannot compete. She is scoffed at. Scorned. Dismissed. Lambasted by other women—working women—who say that her husband cheated with the woman at the office because, as a stay-at-home mom, she could not possibly sate her husband's intellectual curiosity with conversations of preschool curriculum, birthday cake, and idle gossip. That her frivolous days filled with child-rearing, mindless errands, and household chores can in no way compete with the rigors of a working mom's schedule and the dynamic existence her full life gives rise to.

However, is that really the case?

Any stay-at-home mom knows it is not. Yet women continue to tell other women differently. I recently came across an article published by the New York Post last spring discussing how to spot a gold digger. In it, matchmaker Janis Spindel, founder of the high-end matchmaker service Janis Spindel Serious Matchmaking Inc., explains, "My clients need to know that the women are upscale, professional people and they have a job—they don't really care what the job is, but they have to have a real job." As Spindel elaborates, that job needs to pay at least six figures.

Ouch.

By "real," I am assuming she does not mean raising children full time, the job I have held for more than a decade. Because that position, as we all know, does not constitute gainful employment according to the IRS and, if it did, would likely not be of the six-figure variety. Applying Spindel's criteria here, that would mean the stay-at-home mom (presumably now divorced if vying for a spot in her coveted pool of eligible singles), would not be considered a desirable candidate for her match-making service, which prides itself on discerning those women looking for true love from those looking for money, a.k.a. gold diggers, because the stay-at-home mom does not earn her own.

Pretty harsh words, I would say, since most of the stay-at-home moms I know are highly educated, articulate women with varied interests who, though possessing Spindel's qualifying earning potential on paper, either put their earnings on hold or left the workforce early to raise children full time before their earning capacity was fully realized. Women who, using their education and skills, apply their knowledge to make their schools and communities flourish for everyone's benefit, including those women working full time whose schedules do not always allow the same level of contribution. Go to any PTO fundraiser, often run almost entirely by women, and you will see the equivalent of a well-managed, profitable business in action.

As Spindel goes on to illustrate, it is not all that difficult to spot a gold digger. A lack of a job is a telltale sign a woman is looking for someone to support her. "Women must have [jobs]," she elaborates. "It gives them a sense of confidence, allows them to support themselves and keeps them busy during the day."

Um, busy?

Since first becoming a mother, I do not recall many moments when I have not been busy. As for confidence, well, it is sometimes difficult to feel confident when the primary yardstick by which success is measured is money. And that is the real shame in all of this.

The stay-at-home mom's success is arguably not always as easily quantifiable as it is for the woman working outside the home who may receive a commendation from her boss for a stellar performance on a complicated presentation or for the lawyer who wins a high-profile trial on her client's behalf.

Instead, the stay-at-home mom's success comes in those often inconspicuous rewards, such as witnessing the joy on her child's face as the child makes a new friend during a playdate she arranged or the sense of pride her child exudes after doing well on a math test for which she and her child spent hours studying together. And then, sometimes, that reward simply comes from getting through a long day. One that will inevitably lead to yet another long day during which that mom will continue guiding her children into adulthood, to hopefully one day grow into decent people and contributing members of society.

The man I end up with will value those triumphs. He will not see me as a gold digger because I did not support myself during those years when I was married and raising my family. The fact that I have not been gainfully employed in a number of years will not be considered evidence that I do not now desire to be. And he will not assume because I am not employed full time outside the home that I am looking for someone to fill my ex-husband's shoes supporting me.

Staying home to raise children is a personal choice made between a husband and wife in consideration of their family's individual needs and circumstances. It is no more or less noble a decision than that made by a woman who chooses to work full time while doing the same. There are benefits and sacrifices involved in both. However, what women who work outside the home need to stop doing is condemning women who choose differently and then pressuring those women to apologize for the legitimate choices they made.

To anyone who argues that girls run the world, I say absolutely. Only some of us have chosen to run it from our minivans. And that counts too.

On Jacky O'Shaughnessy: Is Baring All Becoming Too Much to Bear?

I'm becoming increasingly frustrated.

With women feeling defensive, myself included, about the beauty of their aging (or aged) bodies. It's all the rage now—women taking it all off, flaunting their bodily imperfections in the name of self-expression. Art, if you will. Then dialoguing about the damage societal perceptions of beauty have caused the psyches of these smart, beautiful females in conjunction with the self-deprecating videos and "artistic" photographs they display.

That's not to say the frustrations of these women aren't legitimate. They most definitely are. The world at large is a tough crowd to please.

I, too, have bought into the self-love wave, although not fully, as I remain a slave to my weekly beauty regimen, trying to attract love into my life in the best and only way that I know how—through my appearance.

I convince myself I'm beautiful despite my flaws. And there are many. I encourage others to do the same for themselves. Yet I continue to fall prey to the pressure of living up to and maintaining an idealistic image of how an attractive woman should look. Because I feel, I *know*, I have no choice despite all the brouhaha about embracing inner beauty.

Imperfectly perfect vaginas, whatever the hell that means.

Therapeutic photography, otherwise known as the only standard by which I will ever be a model.

Celebrations of imperfect bodies, like my own, photographed in dim lighting, pretty vignettes, and at flattering angles.

Calculated portrayals.

I'm in my forties. Divorced. I'm a single mother. I'm flawed. But I'm also in love with love—in love with finding someone to love and with finding someone to love me, the true me.

The evolved version of myself knows I'm doing it wrong. Luring men from the outside in. Maybe that makes me inauthentic. A phony. But I can't stop. Insult and rejection await me if I do. Or, even worse, invisibility.

It's not that I'm bitter or disillusioned. I actually wish I were disillusioned. It's that I'm tired of apologizing. Apologizing for who I am under the pretense of burgeoning self-esteem.

In fact, the exact opposite is true.

As I write this, I'm being asked to forward "sexy" pictures of myself to a forty-five-year-old "gentleman" with whom I'm texting on the dating app Tinder. After rebuking him, I'm being further advised that sending additional photos will be my only hope of securing a date. Dismiss him, and I will have to "just continue to settle for the mediocre losers."

Warning duly noted, sir, but I shall respectfully decline your offer anyway.

Though I can't say that I wasn't tempted to send photos. Only not the ones he was expecting.

That brainchild came to me after watching Jacky O'Shaughnessy's piece for Elisa Goodkind and Lily Mandelbaum's *The What's Underneath Project*, a YouTube series created to celebrate the individual and authentic styles men and women embody when they have grown comfortable in their own skin.

In it, the current face of American Apparel, 62-year-old O'Shaughnessy, slowly undresses for the camera as she bares all, sharing both her physical and emotional vulnerabilities with her internet audience. Describing her then fifty-two-year-old boyfriend's refusal to be seen publicly with her because of her advanced age while dating him five years earlier, it's understandable why she feels compelled to sit in that chair, justifying her worthiness. Her pain is palpable.

I'm here she figuratively waves to the world. Please see me, the real me, we can almost hear her say, though these words never once pass her blood-red lips.

For a moment during a series such as this one, that wish may come true.

That's because each and every one of us is beautiful, O'Shaughnessy and myself included. If we are enlightened enough, we may actually see it for ourselves, in ourselves. Unfortunately for women, too many men do not, despite our protests to the contrary.

I appreciate the intent of this body of work. The message it seeks to convey. The change that it tries to inspire.

But once the cameras fade to black, I'm afraid so, too, does the message.

Because I can guess what the response will be if I send my new pen pal a "sexy" photo of my bare stomach, scarred with stretch marks acquired during three pregnancies, or a seductive shot of myself without my makeup on or my hair not styled. Though I'm proud of and grateful for the work my body has done thus far, I know there are many others who would not share with me that same appreciation.

Poet and playwright Oscar Wilde once said, "Life imitates Art far more than Art imitates Life." I can't say that I disagree. Current standards of beauty and style are, arguably, not always artistic. It's here I agree with Goodkind's contention that the fashion industry has, in many ways, lost its creativity and, hence, its embrace and accurate depiction of individual style. But where I differ is my proposed handling of it.

I say we stop pleading our case. We stop defending ourselves. We stop grandstanding. And we start loving ourselves without seeking the rest of the world's approval.

Then I say grab your camera.

And the next time some middle-aged guy demeans you based on your appearance, point that lens at him and ask that dude to sit squarely on a stool while he undresses and declare to the world how he adores his sagging testicles, thinning hair, and flabby gut.

My guess is he won't be so quick to jump on the band-wagon.

Ladies, please. Get ahold of yourselves. Put your clothes back on and show some self-respect. These endless public displays are becoming no less fictitious than the beauty myths they seek to dispel. Authenticity means living your life knowing who you are and having the courage to do so without exposing yourself to the same scrutiny such efforts are meant to curtail.

With that in mind, I silently bid my digital pen pal farewell. And spoke volumes about myself.

Why Keeping the Faith Is Necessary for Finding the One

I'm Jewish. Born and bred. A living, breathing matzo ball and card-carrying member of Chabad and Hadassah. OK, OK, so maybe I'm embellishing just a smidge, and I'm not really a Hadassah member. But the point is I could be. That's why so many would find it out of character that, notwithstanding the long line of Jewish American princesses from which I hail and staunch devotion to the Jewish faith as evidenced by my sought after brisket and chicken soup at holiday time, the Catholic Church has continued to fascinate me ever since adolescence.

Perhaps my preoccupation began in my "Lawn Guyland" home with my surreptitious and forbidden reading of *The Thorn Birds* as I sat hidden from sight on the burnt orange shag carpet in my parents' walk-in closet, nestled deep within the forest of my father's pinstriped suits and my mother's Cher Bono-esque dresses. And then later continued with my love of any film involving a good old-fashioned exorcism. I mean, what member of the tribe wouldn't be captivated? Although we Jews would probably just find the right doctah to eradicate a pesky ol' case of demonic possession anyway.

My interest in Catholicism lasted well into my adulthood and took me as far as a first date with a Presbyterian minister I matched with on Tinder (shocking, I know, even by Tinder standards), the closest I could ever have come to dating a Catholic priest. Unfortunately for me, although a nice guy, a sexy Father Ralph de Bricassart, my collared friend was not. (No, he didn't wear the collar on our date.)

All kidding aside, the Catholic doctrine that interests me most, even to this day, is the rite of confession. To my knowledge, the Jewish religion offers nothing of the kind. To cope, we stereotypically harbor our sins and then feel guilty about them afterward. Hey, for whatever it's worth, this time-honored tradition has survived for more than 5,000 years and continues to go on strong, as Jewish mothers everywhere can attest.

However, I do believe there is real value in getting feelings off your chest. Bam! Right out into the open. Instead of letting emotions fester and becoming hurt and angry as they do. Go ahead. Try it. Blurt something out. I highly recommend it. Believe me; it's better than getting stuck. Stagnated. I know because that's how I lived during most of my marriage until its cataclysmic end. As I learned the hard way, sticking your head in the sand can mean only one thing: you're going to get sand in your hair. And because you've got to rinse it out sooner or later, I say wash that man right out of your hair—and fast. (Oh, you're just figuring that out now? Of course this is about a man. Isn't it always?)

But alas, because I'm only a wannabe Catholic, there's no confessional booth waiting for me nor an impartial ear that will bear witness to my sins during times of need. Only a dressing room at Bloomingdale's and my Jewish mother reminding me with pointed finger that any regret I feel for hanging on so long was my own doing because I'm the one who chose to go "back in the fold" (some strange colloquialism that has to do with following the rest of the herd or, in this case, harem) over and over again with a guy who, after the first few months of dating, claimed he never misrepresented his intentions toward me (and, I can only presume, many others).

She was right.

Though it should've been conceivable, that understanding was still not enough, and one ordinary day I professed my former feelings in a text. So high school, I know. Here I paraphrase: I was in love with you, and you never truly cared.

And guess what? After I hit send, I felt a sudden release like I had never experienced before. It was such a rush that I almost followed up my confessional text with another to share my exuberance. I said almost.

You may be wondering, was I sorry afterward?

Buyer's remorse is a feeling with which I'm intimately familiar. My American Express card can vouch for that, having seen more than its fair share of returns during my shopping heyday pre-divorce. But as I re-read my confession seconds, hours, and even days later, I had no regrets. I still don't. Nope. Not a one.

What he said, or didn't say, in response is of no consequence. I was finally done, once and for all. Set free by my own accord, by my own big mouth, the only way I could ever have been set free. My only sin was having waited so long.

Love is a gift. How we love—and who we give that love to—says more about us than it does the other person. That said, I don't think we can ever choose who we love. When we fall in love—and that love is reciprocated—it's pure magic.

This wasn't.

What I do believe is that we can choose whether we continue to love. When we love someone who doesn't love us in return—at least not in the way that we want or deserve—who doesn't treat us well and who doesn't make us feel good, we cannot love with all our heart. So we don't actually love; we pine.

Which means all along that we haven't been open to meeting the one we're meant to love, the one who will love us back wholeheartedly. Perhaps it's because we weren't yet ready. Perhaps it's because the timing wasn't quite right. Perhaps it's because we simply hadn't met him yet. I'm not entirely sure.

But what I do know for certain is that it's important to have faith. Not only in him (whoever he may be) but also in ourselves. Because you and me? We're worthy of love and so much more.

Forgive me, Mother, for I have sinned. I hankered for a man who didn't want me, and I behaved like a schmuck. I'm sure as a mother that was painful to watch.

I hope you can forgive me because I've forgiven myself. And finally moved on.

Chance Encounters and Waiting for the One Who Likes Me Just as I Am

"It is a truth universally
acknowledged that when one
part of your life starts going
OK, another falls spectacu-
larly to pieces." —Bridget,
Bridget Jones's Diary, 2001

You know those bad date stories we women all love to talk about? The ones I love to talk about? Well, this past Saturday night, I turned the tables—on myself—and became someone else's bad date. I had the best of intentions. I did.

I swear to God the night was cosmically charged or something. For disaster. Maybe. I hope not. Although I'm kind of beginning to think so because as the clock ticks, I'm growing more and more doubtful that I'll ever hear from this person again and that I'll be forced to resign the evening to one I'd like to forget. No, strike that. One I'd like to do all over again but know I will never have the chance to.

It's almost as if I brought it on myself. Like, what kind of idiot goes trudging into the city for a first date in the middle of a snowstorm? This idiot, of course. The woman who spends her life looking for the one. The one that I like to think is somewhere out there waiting to meet me. I'm such a dreamer that before I left my house, an image of Renée Zellweger kissing Colin Firth in the falling snow at the end of *Bridget Jones's Diary* popped into my head. Dreamer, I know, with a big fat capital D.

I've been chasing this elusive one for a while now, looking for that single, irresistible guy to whisk me away into a world of slow seduction, everlasting love, and, of course, amazing sex.

The reality, is on most dates, I feel nothing. No connection. Nada. Zilch. Sometimes my date feels something, and if I'm not altogether ambivalent, then, of course, I get swept away, sort of, and chase the feeling the guy is having, hoping, praying, that I can behold it one day for myself. "Maybe," I think, "I missed it." So I "investigate" by seeing that person again. Sometimes even again after that. Depends on how not ambivalent I really am.

Then other times, though more infrequently, I'm "lucky" enough to wind up "in" a relationship that I know, in my heart of hearts, isn't right. Too often, I stay longer than I should, trying to turn that relationship into something it's not and somehow justify the time I've already invested. All the while feeling frustrated because I know it's not the relationship I want. Or deserve.

Naturally, I have felt "it" too. Whatever that is—chemistry, lust, intense connection—right along with the other person. At which point, some type of relationship ensues, though, as of now, not one that has lasted.

As I walked through slushy streets in expensive boots not meant for snow, in freezing temperatures, to get to the restaurant after my regular dating "commute" on the train into New York City, I began thinking that there must be a reason why I didn't stay home. I even texted my date about an hour before leaving to make sure he still wanted to go to the trouble. He did if I did.

"I'm fearless," I joked, agreeing to meet.

But was that the case?

When I got to the restaurant, I was met by this cute guy in his early forties. Not the self-centered, emotionally unavailable power-monger type I usually gravitate to. Different. A little more . . . zen. Spiritual. As it turns out, more like me. Because, at my old age of forty-two, I've finally realized why I didn't always fit into my own life—I was a little bit more creative than I let on. Crunchier than I looked. Perceptive.

I stifled that identity for years, deferring to the straitlaced, Type A personality everyone thought I had and linear thinker everyone thought I was. Or, probably more accurately, everyone thought I should be.

I led what many would call a charmed life with the applicable accoutrements. All good, except that my life didn't quite fit with my spirit and over time began to squash it, until the day when my cover was finally blown to smithereens.

I'm normally a good date. I am. I'm what you would call a seasoned date. Not that I always was. I most certainly wasn't. But now that I've been doing this for a little while, I'm usually confident. Smart. Funny. Some might even say witty. Because of that, I usually "get the guy." At least I do for a while, as in a call back after the interview.

However, I don't function well under pressure, so I like to get to my destination early and compose myself. Which would've been nice, especially that night, since I got there and was shivering, had wet feet, and was feeling slightly disheveled as a result. But I was ten minutes late, and I didn't get my requisite prep time. I excused myself to the ladies' room to pull myself together as best I could.

When I returned, we sat down at our table. Within moments, I began yapping away nervously, oblivious to my surroundings, telling my life story that, of course, included my ex-husband. I wasn't saying anything negative about him. I'm beyond that. These days, we get along well. But it was my version and not a conversation I would imagine having in front of my ex-husband, let alone while on a first date. But, essentially, that's what, unbeknownst to me, I was doing.

Never once did I look around me. I was just so self-absorbed. And absorbed in talking to this guy. But about ten minutes in, I happened to look to my left at the people sitting next to me, the ones sitting in total silence at the next table.

"Wow," I thought, "the guy sitting only inches away from me looks familiar." I looked to see who he was sitting with and immediately recognized my ex-husband's niece. By the looks on their faces, it was clear she and her fiancé had seen me there the whole time but never said hello.

Our eyes met. And the awkward hellos began to fly. As if that weren't enough, I scanned the rest of their table and also noticed my ex-husband's nephew and his significant other sitting there too. No one had bothered to let me know they were there.

I introduced everyone to my date and then proceeded to mouth to my date that we needed to move to a different table, texting him like an immature high school girl the reason why. No way could I talk to him freely with an audience, especially since we didn't know each other well.

I said my hellos and then my goodbyes to everyone at the table, gave an honest explanation as to why I could no longer sit there, and moved. All good. Right? Not really. Now I was even more flustered.

To put me at ease, my date told me I was meant to meet him and that this chance meeting with my ex-husband's family was supposed to happen, that there was definitely a reason. I only needed to figure out what it was. After all, what were the odds that I would sit down next to them in a restaurant of his choosing in the middle of Manhattan on the night of a snowstorm?

As I now recount the night's events, none of this sounds like a big deal. In truth, it isn't. So what. So my ex-husband's family saw me on a date. They've seen my ex-husband, their uncle, with another woman for years. So his family might have eavesdropped on my conversation. Not cool, but at the end of the day, who cares.

I did. But the question was, why?

My date proposed that I'm not over my ex-husband. In fact, nothing could be further from the truth. If he appeared at my doorstep looking to reconcile, I would never agree. Oh, I've forgiven him for cheating on me, all right. But there's no way I could ever go back to our passionless marriage.

Perhaps, my date alternatively suggested, this was some kind of message to my ex-husband that I had moved on. Doubtful. He wouldn't care if I had or had not, and I'm fine with that too.

Honestly, after I thought about it, I had the answer all along. It turned out I had sent it into the universe myself, via text, taunting whatever higher power there is that I was the person I purported to be.

Of my willingness to travel in the snow, I had texted my date that I was fearless before leaving home to meet him that evening. Right after I sent it, I looked at the text, thinking, "Where did that come from?" The universe, it seemed, wanted to know as well. And it wasn't the first time the universe had asked.

Two weeks earlier, I had this question posed to me on another first date: "Are you ready for someone to love you?"

I replied that I was. No, it wouldn't be that guy, as I would discover days later when he texted to say he had decided not to pursue a relationship with me. But the question was nonetheless intriguing.

Not long before that, a mentor of mine suggested I'm uncoupled because I want to be. "No," I adamantly disagreed. That is until I thought about it.

For a long time, what she said was, indeed, correct. Though I've dated—a lot—and have had relationships, they were always with people who treated me like the fox that I was. The fox who relished taking a running jump to swipe at grapes which were always just out of reach, at relationships with men who I knew couldn't and wouldn't give me the meaningful relationship I professed to want.

I now realize I had been afraid. Afraid of finally letting go of the past and outing myself to the world—the entire world—without feeling self-conscious.

The Rule of Three tells us that the energy we send into the universe will come back to us threefold. The events of last Saturday night more than qualify. On that night, my two worlds finally collided to become one.

Unfortunately, my earlier suspicion proved correct, and I've just learned that my date and I will not be moving forward together. I'm disappointed, but I agree we met for a reason, and it was a worthwhile one.

Pre-Date Etiquette: Forging Intimacy Through Text

We just broke up. I'm doing OK, though, so please, don't worry about me. The relationship wasn't long, and I know in my heart that I will be able to recover with time.

He told me he was thinking about me. Wished me sweet dreams on the nights he promised to call but didn't. In the end, he asked me if I had disappeared, moved on. I felt it best to not respond, although I know it may sound harsh.

Why be so cold, so seemingly callous? Because, in fact, we never met. Never spoke on the phone, not even once. Ours was a relationship based entirely on texts. Mostly his.

We met online, of course, in the place where nobody knows your name (cue *Cheers* theme song). A chance meeting in cyberspace. He sent me a "Flirt," and I deemed his somewhat normal-looking profile the one out of over a hundred I received during my first week on this particular dating site worthy of a response.

The email exchange was brief, kept deliberately short by me. I'm not looking for a pen pal, after all, and I don't believe in wasting anyone's time, especially my own. He asked for my number, and I obliged.

"Call u tonite," he promised. "Happy Monday."

No call followed, however. Only an apology text late that night for blowing me off. "Got home really late," was the chosen explanation.

"Happy Tuesday!" chimed my iPhone early the next morning. Will "try to reach you 6:30-7:30" on the drive home from work.

No call ever came, though, only another text suggesting that a 9 p.m. call would be too late considering I have to put my daughter to bed.

"Daughter?" I questioned.

My eldest daughter is in the eighth grade, my second daughter in the seventh, and both rarely fall asleep before 11 p.m. Funny, I didn't recall ever discussing my children's sleep habits with this stranger.

"Sorry, meant son and daughter."

"OK," I thought, "I have two daughters *and* a son, jackass. Now you're clearly confusing me with someone else."

But I'm a good sport, so I suggested that if he wanted to still call around nine, that would be fine. He agreed. But . . . he never called. Only texted again, this time claiming he was confused. He thought I was supposed to call him!

"Whoops," he bellowed over text.

This time, I didn't respond.

Other texts followed over the next three days, solidifying the relationship that never was. Wednesday was an apology for not texting me all day ("big meeting in Massachusetts"), Thursday was a wish for a "Happy 'Thump Day'" (this guy sure likes the days of the week), along with more well wishes for a good day at work (I'm a stay-at-home mom, my work day never ends). And then came Friday, breakup day ("Did u disappear? Move on already?").

Yes, it was true. I had disappeared. I had moved on. But probably not like he thought. I wasn't "onto the next," like so many online serial daters are today. On that day, I moved on to me.

Finding someone special means putting our best foot forward. So to any man who doesn't? I'm happy to say, these days, all I can give you is the boot.

Spiritual but Not Religious:
Ambiguous Online Dating Profiles
and Self-Loathing Jews

"I'm actually Jewish."

The faith question had been left conspicuously blank in his Match.com profile. Based on experience, I assumed why. Yet I can never be certain until I learn otherwise. But as I heard those familiar words during our first phone call, a self-deprecating confession of sorts, I felt just a wee bit excited with this added knowledge. Like Judy Benjamin did in the 1980 comedic film *Private Benjamin* when she learned Dr. Henri Alan Tremont, her sexy French love interest, was Jewish. Then, and only then, did she agree to sleep with him.

Pay dirt.

I don't know what it is but I, like Judy Benjamin, am a sucker for a handsome Jewish man. Not that I haven't dated non-Jewish guys before. I have. And I'm open to meeting men of other religions. But I do list in my profile openly and proudly, I might add, that I'm Jewish.

Yes, I realize on a secular site like Match.com I'm exposing myself to rejection from those who want to date only women of their own faith, and that's perfectly fine. Everyone is entitled to see whomever he or she wants. Yes, my candor does occasionally subject me to such left-handed compliments as "You're too beautiful to be Jewish." But the choice of how to react remains mine.

Delete.

More than a few Jewish guys have revealed to me how they are either apathetic about their faith or don't like to date Jewish women at all. When I hear such preemptive statements or witness outright efforts to masquerade Jewish descent, I stop and wonder what causes these men to feel such shame.

I admit I'm not religious. I don't keep a kosher home and have zero desire to do so. I rarely attend synagogue, not even on High Holy Days. And I eat shellfish and pork with wild abandon.

Sue me.

I'm spiritual, though, but not *not* Jewish enough to classify myself under the Match.com catchphrase "Spiritual but not religious." I firmly believe religious faith, whichever faith it might be, plays a large part in picking a potential partner, regardless of whether it is the first, second, or umpteenth time around. Apart from the logistics of being entrenched in organized religion, i.e., dietary rules, chosen houses of worship, and the specific scripture from which we pray, a long history of traditions and values should be thoughtfully considered and not readily dismissed.

Interfaith marriages can be successful; I don't deny that and have witnessed those of friends and family. But achieving such integration requires first taking pride in our identity. And then, through education and learning, gaining an understanding of what it is we choose to renounce or embrace.

I'm confounded by the apparent sense of self-loathing exhibited by so many Jews. Faith is only one part of who we are.

Religious identity should be worn with pride, not fear or shame. If a potential match doesn't want to be with us because of our beliefs, revealing them later will likely make little, if any, difference. Not to mention, it raises the more pressing question: why would we want to be with a person who doesn't want to be with us?

Own up. Be proud. There are a lot of women out there looking for a mensch. And there are a lot of men who would be only too happy to find themselves a balabusta. Leaving out information or hiding behind ambiguous titles only postpones what will eventually be or not be.

So feel free to tick that "Jewish" box. You're not bragging. You're kvelling.

Love Triangle or Bermuda Triangle? Depends on Who You Ask

Not long ago, I was dating someone I sort of liked. But when he and I began making each other crazy, and it began to fall apart, I thought it time to start redirecting my attention back online.

As I sifted through old emails from guys I had placed on the back burner should precisely this scenario arise (as it so often does and will until it won't), I grumbled to myself why finding my dream guy has to be this difficult.

After answering messages from some contenders, I took another moment to peruse the ~~mug shots~~ headshots on the Jdate "Members Online" page. That's when I spotted him: a mid-forties, tall, cute, educated professional with a lifestyle and interests similar to mine. Poifect! The only problem, if you want to call it one, was that he lived locally.

Because . . . I. Don't. Do. That. (I've since reconsidered and am willing to give up my dating "commute" once and for all.)

True, I've dated plenty. But most of the guys have been out-of-towners, mainly because of dumb luck, and also because I haven't really gone looking for love in all the "right" places—in my own neighborhood where I would have a better chance of sustaining a meaningful relationship. What can I say? I like my privacy (notwithstanding the fact that I write a dating blog).

This guy, however, lived only fifteen minutes away in one of the towns neighboring my own, one in the trifurcate of incestuously Jewish locales here in good ol' suburban New Jersey where we all date each other.

I looked long and hard at the guy's photo. Then back again at his profile. I got nothing. Bupkis. No bells went a ringing.

So I did the unthinkable. That is, for a rules (as in Ellen Fein and Sherrie Schneider's *The Rules: Time-Tested Secrets for Capturing the Heart of Mr. Right*) girl like. me, a girl who believes, and still does, that a man must pursue. That a man must lead. But hey, the God of all gods, dating coach Evan Marc Katz, says it's OK for women to email first. And I've read more of his dating blog than I have the Bible, which is why I decided to listen to him and take what he said as gospel (even though E.M.K. and I are both Jewish).

Technically, I guess that makes this all sort of his fault. But E.M.K. is as cute as could be, and I love his dating advice (apart from this dastardly tip), so I won't hold it against him. Not for long, anyhow.

I don't need to tell you what happened next. I typed a short, flirty email. Yes. I. Did. And suddenly, I went from dating like Elizabeth Walton to dating like Elizabeth Hurley (in my mind, at least).

Wouldn't you know, he answered me!

We exchanged more short emails that afternoon. Then he asked if I would by any chance be available to meet for a drink that night, being that we live so close.

My mind began to race, and my heart began to pound.

He could be a serial killer! After all, the Craigslist killer was Jewish. And a doctor, no less! Well, almost. He was still in medical school. Same difference. That means the odds of a Jewish consultant also being a serial killer are equally as great, right?

I know those *Rules* ladies would've said setting up a date without the requisite three days advance notice is an absolute no-no. I was pretty sure E.M.K. wouldn't approve of it either.

But since he wasn't on my speed dial because I'm not a paying client (yet), I enlisted the advice of my BFF, who may have known a lot about dating back in the day but who arguably knows less about it now.

"Just go. Be spontaneous!" she ill-advised. "Talk to him on the phone first to see if he sounds weird."

One quick call later, I detected no weirdness whatsoever, and we agreed to meet at this local bar in town where I hate going on dates because I'm sure to (and have) run into my cousin, my friends, and my teenage babysitter's mother all while out on a date.

That night, of course, would be no exception. Which, as it turned out, proved to be the least of my problems.

Our date got off to a good start and was going well. Actually, it was going better than well. So well that I didn't even glance down at my phone to read the barrage of incoming texts. Not the text from my guy friend sitting at a table right behind me who texted to say hi or from my BFF who wanted to make sure I wasn't lying dead in a gutter somewhere, slain by the bare hands of my Jdate.

Now, in all honesty, my vision is pretty abysmal these days. Too many hours spent with my nose buried in a book or in front of a computer screen mean I can't see jack (no, his name wasn't Jack) without my level 2.0 reading glasses sitting squarely on the edge of my nose. Not necessarily the sexiest of looks, and definitely unnecessarily aging. Which is why I left them off and didn't read my BFF's texts that were becoming more frantic by the moment. All I knew was that the texts weren't from my kids, which was good enough for me.

It's also why my BFF convinced herself I was in the process of being tied up somewhere (and not in a good way) and called our mutual friend in a panic.

Meanwhile, as my date and I got chummier, we exchanged all the details people usually do on a first phone call, which we didn't do since ours was so last minute and so short. It was only when I asked that last question, "What does your ex do for a living?" that it all came together or, I should say, fell apart.

Just like that, I became Daphne in a *Scooby-Doo, Where are You!* episode, watching as my date's true identity was revealed. My mind flashed back through all of the "clues" I should have picked up on earlier but hadn't, clues which all would have led me to the conclusion that I was on a date with . . .

wait for it . . .

my friend's ex.

OMFG!

I was out to lunch with some other friends and her just days earlier. Her ex even called while we were at the restaurant, a call she sent straight to voicemail because he wanted to go over the last remaining details of their divorce agreement before finalizing it.

My jaw dropped.

He looked at me like, "WTF?"

So I asked. And he confirmed. Yep, he was my friend's ex.

And then it dawned on me: "Hey, wait a minute, you told me you're divorced!"

"Well, I have what's known as a get," he began to lecture. "You know, a Jewish divorce."

I rolled my eyes.

How the hell was I going to explain this one to my friend, I wondered, as well as to my other friends who are also her friend? I could already hear the *Beverly Hills, 90210*-type phone conversation playing out in my mind:

Hi, Brenda. This is Kelly. I just want to let you know I started dating Dylan right after we went out to lunch last week for your birthday.

My crazy train, however, was interrupted by something even crazier. At that very moment, the bartender approached us and said there was an urgent call waiting for me at the other end of the bar from my friend who was locked out of her house and needed her key.

OK, I know I've been to this place a lot. But this local establishment isn't Cheers, and my name isn't Norm. No way should I be receiving calls there. Ever. Besides, I didn't have anyone else's house key.

I picked up the phone. "Hello?"

"Act natural," a familiar but brusque voice ordered.

Suddenly I was involved in a covert operation I knew nothing about.

"BFF and I want to make sure you're OK since you didn't answer any of her texts. BFF is convinced you're out with a serial killer!"

No such luck.

"I'm fine," I said. "Really."

But, to be honest, I wasn't all that sure. So when I got back to my seat, I methodically explained who had called—a friend on behalf of another friend (who also both happen to be friends with his almost ex)—and how they were worried about me because I was with him, despite not knowing who "him" actually was.

After discussing it, we decided not to tell anyone we had gone on a date. Other than that, there was nothing to tell—yet—and if eventually there was information about a romance worth sharing, we would.

But the next morning, I called "Brenda" anyway. I couldn't have it any other way. It simply didn't feel right, even if it was only one date.

She listened and was not only understanding but encouraging as well.

"I would *love* for you to be my kids' stepmom," she gushed.

Hold up, sister.

She wasn't quite as enthusiastic after our second date when she broke things off with me for him. Yes, you read that correctly. My date's ex-wife (their divorce was finalized sometime during all of the mishigas) informed me that her ex-husband and I would no longer be dating. As she put it, although he liked me, he thought seeing one of her friends might be weird.

Perhaps she was right. That said, I didn't think it would be as weird as this conversation was.

Hey, it's probably all for the best. Even though Brenda and Dylan were already apart, no one ever totally forgave Kelly.

The Witches NOT of Eastwick, and Who I Went Home with on Date Night

It was my fourth date this week. As I dressed for the evening, wearing my standard first date attire—tight black pants, black boots, and a sexy but not so sexy top—I said a quick prayer that tonight would be the reward for the three shitty dates that came before it. I was beginning to worry that I was losing my touch. Alas, within seconds of meeting him and seeing that he looked like a bad version of his Tinder profile picture, the disappointment came crashing in.

I ordered a drink, a ginger ale, because I didn't want to even risk that alcohol could somehow cloud my judgment here, although I'm pretty certain one drink wouldn't have been enough to do the trick. Instead, I thought to myself how I would've rather been at home watching a movie in my pajamas on the couch. Screw Saturday night. I was over it. Way over. It was official. I had finally reached saturation, the point where I would've rather been home than out on a date.

The conversation was boring, and I already felt a headache coming on. No, not really, but I was secretly wishing for one, giving me the legitimate excuse I needed to leave. So when he asked me if I would like to join him for dinner, I politely declined, informing him that I already ate. (See, guys, not all women are looking for a free meal.)

The minutes dragged on, each one feeling longer than the one before it. Honestly, I never intended to be that girl. Never wanted to be that girl. Yet my mind continued to wander to strategies about how best to make my escape.

Recently a friend described a necklace currently on the market that can be programmed to call a specific phone number with the quick push of an inconspicuous button. One press and in comes the call from your "friend" telling of the emergency to which you must turn your attention. Unfortunately for me, as I pressed down hard on the diamond pendant around my neck, nothing happened.

"Damn," I hissed under my breath, "I should've bought the thing when I had the chance."

But, like a gift from God, like manna from heaven, a notification of a tweet vibrated my phone. I looked at it as if it were an urgent message from the Oval Office itself and furrowed my brow.

"Ugh, this isn't good," I said, feigning distress while bringing the tips of my left index and middle fingers to my right temple. I looked down at my drink. Then, noticing it was still half full, picked it up, chugged it back, and stood.

I offered my excuses (headache plus exhaustion) at the same time as reaching for my coat, which I had folded neatly over the back of the stool next to me just in case I needed to make a quick getaway.

He seemed disappointed. Perhaps hurt. Sure, I would've also felt crappy if someone had done that to me. Fortunately, it hasn't happened—yet—but I can only imagine when it does. After all, every ~~dog~~ bitch has her day.

However, I didn't necessarily think I was being a bitch. Although I'm pretty sure this story will go down in the annals and one day be rattled off to a future date of his, the tale about how this rude woman just got up and left him at the bar after only twenty minutes.

I've heard tales of woe like this before, so I know I'm not alone. But that's the price you pay for misrepresenting yourself in the photos in your online dating profile and why I never do it. Looking your best is one thing, not accurately portraying who you are another.

Once in the car, I called my friend who, only thirty minutes earlier, had wished me good luck on my date. Good luck, my ass. If there is such a thing, I sure wasn't feeling it. She and another mutual friend were about to leave for the evening. Girls' night out or group therapy, as I like to say. Just what the doctor ordered. I was in.

Minutes later, I was sitting in the back of my friend's car on my way to some new trendy restaurant and bar. We were quite a crew. Sexless in the suburbs; one of us dealing with a recent breakup, another cursing the fiancée of her ex-boyfriend/love of her life, and me, a runaway date.

Upon arrival, the night looked promising. Gourmet food, upscale bar, possibly (hopefully) some cute guys. And then we found one—for the three of us. Aren't those usually the odds for us middle-agers?

What this guy must have been thinking! Damn, I blame the alcohol. We had to have sounded like the women in the 1987 blockbuster film *The Witches of Eastwick* as we vied for his attention.

"I just bought a house!"

"I went to law school!"

"You really like my boobs?"

"I have perky boobs too!"

"My ass is cute, isn't it? *Isn't it?*"

"I am general counsel of the world!"

Who was going to get him, this cute forty-eight-year-old smart, successful single dad? He was a little short for me and not Jewish, but I was willing to make an exception. A compromise. See? I ditched the list. Truly, I did. I've even started dating men without an MBA.

As we sipped our drinks, reveling in our good fortune, he stepped away for a moment. And, then, like hens . . .

"Who do you think he likes?" we whispered in hushed tones, the vodka already taking ahold of our reason. Each of us pointed to the other so as not to insult.

"He likes you!"

"No, he likes you!"

While what we were really thinking was, "It's me, me, me!"

Fools.

He returned to the table moments later, and that's when he dropped the bomb: he had a girlfriend. He had just gone to call her.

I reached over, pulled my phone from my bag, and began checking emails. Next, I went to pee. Game over. We all lost. Another night down the toilet.

Or was it?

When I came back, well, that's when all the fun started. That's when we let our hair down. Way down.

"Wow," he commented as the profanity began to fly. "What happened here?"

"What *happened*?" I asked, rolling my eyes. Men are so oblivious sometimes.

"You're no longer a prospect," I explained, wise beyond my limited time on the dating scene.

So we laughed. One of us even cried. (No, not me. Not this time, at least.) We talked about relationships. Sex. Size. Positions. Orgasms. He claimed his girlfriend had eight with him just the other night. Eight!

I'll have what she's having!

Then the check came. And this dude paid. PAID! For all of us! Guys, listen up. This. Is. How. It's. Done. We offered, really we did. But he wouldn't take it.

And then . . .

He took the three of us up to his apartment.

Oh. Yes. He. Did.

Stud muffin. How cool for him. He got to walk out of a bar with three middle-aged beyotches on his arm.

Upstairs we . . .

Played with his dogs. Contemplated his art. And critiqued how he decorated his swanky apartment.

Then we left. Together. My friends and I.

After the girls and I parted ways for the night, I was left alone with my thoughts. I had had high hopes for the evening.

Every new date offers a chance at happiness sharing my life with someone else. But as I came home to my house, my empty bedroom, and got into my king-size bed, alone, I felt good. Beautiful. Desired, even though no man desired me that night.

And I slept like a baby, comforted that my friends would be there for me in the morning.

Aesop's 'The Cock and The Jewel': An Allegory for Modern Dating

A cock goes in search of food. Swiping at the ground, he uncovers a beautiful gem. Not knowing what to do with it, he casts it aside, preferring one grain of barleycorn to all the jewels in the world.

In a similar way . . .

A cock goes in search of, ahem, feline. Swiping at his smartphone, he uncovers a beautiful cougar. Not knowing what to do with her, he casts her aside, preferring one kitten (or many) to all the cougars in the world.

Is this simple allegory a statement on the value of older women as potential partners? I like to think not. Yet the reality is dating a mature and experienced woman, a cougar, especially one with school-aged children needing a lot of attention, is not always the most appealing prospect to a man similarly situated with his own parental obligations or to a man who never had or no longer has any of his own.

It's ironic because, in my early forties, one failed marriage and three children later, I prefer the way I look now to how I did ten years ago. Today, I'm also more self-assured than I ever was during my marriage. And confidence radiates.

That said, dating during my late thirties and early forties has been a struggle. Not for finding dates, but for eventually moving forward into a long-term, committed relationship in which my partner and myself are able to look to each other for emotional comfort and support. To be clear, by commitment, I don't mean exclusivity alone, one important aspect of commitment but certainly not the only. Commitment exists in the mind, in addition to the body, and cannot be feigned.

When a man enters a relationship with a woman who has children, another man's children, he may legitimately have concerns. Beyond financial obligations, which may or may not become his, there are emotional obligations he will need to assume. Committing to an entire family is a serious undertaking and, in earnest, not for everyone.

And that's OK. Better to know sooner than later a man's intentions and capabilities.

As for what "kind" of man will want to assume such a commitment? This is a question many women seek to answer. The truth of the matter is no one really knows. Many women, particularly those in my age group who have lived, loved, and learned, develop their lists of don'ts. Don't date a man who is separated. Don't date a man who is recently divorced. Don't date a man who has young children. Don't date a man who has no children. Don't, don't, don't.

To that, I say, continue saying "don't," and you will never say "I do" because as far as I can tell, too many don'ts don't add up to much. At middle age, with half a life's experience behind us, who can possibly fit the bill?

The obvious question thus becomes, who should I date?

Although I didn't want to admit it at first, I, too, had a list. Deal breakers. So really, it should come as no surprise to me that I continued to date the same type of man over and over again with little success. The Narcotics Anonymous definition of insanity, that "insanity is repeating the same mistakes and expecting different results," really does hold true.

In the spirit of change, I've recently opened my mind and, accordingly, my search to include men with interests and backgrounds differing from my own. Hopefully, that will bring me one day closer to opening my heart.

Women like to speculate how best to catch a man. Make him commit. Indeed, the best way to catch a man is simply not to. A man who wants to devote himself to one woman will. He will appreciate the risk and effort involved, whatever her situation may be. But, more importantly, he will recognize the reward of having not only one to love and love him but more than one.

So the next time some "cock" shies away from commitment, don't get angry. Don't blame him. Thank him. Because the moral of the story is: "Precious things are without value to those who cannot prize them."

Really, you never wanted him anyway. You just hadn't realized it yet.

Shot Down Again, and You're to Blame . . . Gold Diggers, You Give Dating a Bad Name

It's time for a smackdown, ladies. You know who you are. You're the beyotches who use guys for your own personal gain and make the rest of us suffer for it.

I'm talking about those of you who specify which expensive restaurant you want to be taken to on a date and, even more obnoxiously, on a first date. I'm talking about you ladies who hint or even come right out and ask for gifts, gifts such as designer clothing, luxury handbags, and jewelry. I'm talking about you women who demand your parking be paid, taxi fare reimbursed, or babysitting expenses subsidized. No wonder guys are gun-shy about dating. They probably believe most women are gold diggers.

The problem is a lot of women are.

Sadly, men have artilleries of ammunition to back up their suspicions. In 2011, *Business Insider* profiled a twenty-three-year-old New Yorker named Jessica Sporty, who sought to supplement her annual $45,000 salary by joining Match.com and scheduling five dates per week to garner free drinks and dinners.

She maintained a spreadsheet to keep track of the men she dated, and she never dated one particular man more than five times, underscoring her true relationship goals, or lack thereof.

Dinners ranged from casual to upscale and supplemented Jessica's income by approximately $1,200 a month. As news of Jessica's business venture spread, the backlash from men was, understandably, harsh.

Dating websites such as seekingarrangement.com and whatsyourprice.com capitalize on the quid pro quo where men are willing to provide material goods and lifestyle in exchange for the company of beautiful women. The difference is individuals utilizing these sites are complicit in the type of relationship they are pursuing.

Jessica's story may represent an extreme case of exploitation. But I have heard over and over from men I have dated, from male friends, even my own brother, about women taking advantage of their generosity. So what do these opportunists ultimately reap from such bad behavior, besides the obvious monetary benefits? Jaded men who believe women are users and assume a nice night out should be rewarded with sex.

More frustrating is when these women, wide-eyed and innocent, dare to question where all the good men have gone, leaving those of us women who actually desire a real relationship searching for the proverbial needle in a haystack.

Make no mistake. I'm a huge proponent of chivalry, which I believe is a dying art these days. I'm also a traditionalist when it comes to gender roles, at least at the beginning of a relationship.

But I pay my dues too. And those dues ain't cheap.

I, like most people, live on a budget, and dating is an expensive proposition, especially when I date in Manhattan, as I often do. Because I have full physical custody of my children, it's easier for me to travel to my date. But first, I must hire a babysitter, which, in my area, costs between $15 and $20 an hour. Including travel time, I'm usually gone for approximately six hours, sometimes longer. Childcare, therefore, runs between $90 and $120 for the night—plus the cost of the babysitter's dinner, usually takeout. And this is all just so that I can walk out the door!

Thankfully, I have a devoted mother and stepfather who pick up a lot of the slack by frequently coming to visit the kids so I can go out without breaking the bank. But many other women aren't as lucky.

Once I'm on my way, I purchase either a round-trip train ticket (unless I can borrow a train pass from a friend) or drive to the city and incur the cost of gas, tolls, and, if I can't find parking (I'm parallel parking challenged), pay to park in a garage. In total, a date in Manhattan can run me nearly $200. Do that once or twice a week, the expense becomes significant.

But I never say a word. Why? I consider it the cost of doing business, and I'm in the business of finding someone wonderful. My time is valuable, but, unlike my travel expenses, it can't be quantified.

Dating means precious moments spent away from my family. Therefore, while apart from my children, I do look for a means to an end. However, the end isn't a fancy dinner or a new handbag. Rather, the end is a nice evening spent with an intelligent, interesting, and kind person who, hopefully, will feel the same way about me.

Unfortunately, what I'm often met with is a date who, sight unseen, has already sized me up as a gold digger and only wants to be with someone earning big bucks. As a result, I have been on a number of dates with men who felt compelled to announce their yearly incomes. Talk about uncomfortable. I always believed such matters to be private. Perhaps I resembled an IRS auditor they once knew.

On the flip side, I dated a guy for two months who confided his fears about being unable to provide me with the same lifestyle my ex-husband had. As I minimized the importance of money to me, he laughed.

More recently, I had a first and, not coincidentally, last date with a man who insisted I was looking for someone less entrepreneurial and more job stable than himself. I was deeply offended and accused him of projecting his own insecurities onto me. He, in turn, claimed his analysis of my body language revealed disappointment with his livelihood. He said he had been "down that path before," and it wasn't a great one.

Wow. All that from an hour meeting at Starbucks. Perhaps I had unleashed his untapped desire to be a CIA operative. Or, at a minimum, he was a devoted fan of the TV series *Homeland*.

Yet his concern about being down that path before gave me pause. Such defensiveness comes from somewhere. My guess is it came from years of dating conniving women.

My ex-husband has always been generous with money. It's how he expresses affection and what he (erroneously, at least for me) believes brings women happiness. As my marriage neared its end, all that remained were his vacant gifts. One of the last things he bought me was a designer wallet just days before he left. I remember standing in our master bedroom, transferring the contents of my old wallet into the new one, feeling completely alone and unloved. This was not the relationship I wanted. I just didn't know how to leave.

I'm a girl and a girly girl at that. I admit I like nice things. Pretty things. But material objects mean absolutely nothing without sentiment and are a far distant second in priority to a loving relationship.

So ladies, be careful what you wish for. Your walk-in closets won't keep you warm at night. As for the Louis Vuitton luggage that you covet? I'm pretty sure heaven won't accept carry-on bags either. All of it will need to be checked right at the pearly gates.

Is Alimony 'All in the Family'?

Sometimes I am convinced the United Kingdom's 1997 handover of Hong Kong back to the People's Republic of China was a less involved process than the typical handover of my children to their father at vacation time.

I am now in the process of preparing my kids to go on a weeklong vacation with their father over winter break. Because he doesn't live in the United States and doesn't maintain a residence here, the responsibility of preparing our children, emotionally and otherwise, rests solely on me. And my ex is A-OK with that. After all, it's my job. Or at least, that's what he believes.

Every month, I receive alimony which, I am pretty sure to my ex, means I am still on his payroll as I was during our sixteen-year marriage.

"You will never live as my wife again," my ex once raged at me during a heated argument after we had separated.

"Is that a threat or a promise?" I retorted.

So why then, after the finalization of our divorce, am I still being called upon as though I am the dutiful and yet still unappreciated wife?

I am frequently asked to pick up his prescriptions at the pharmacy, send packages to him, make phone calls on his behalf, and purchase sundries for our children in preparation for his family vacations. However, the most egregious request came this past summer when he rented a beach house with his significant other (once upon a time his mistress) and our children and requested I supply all of the children's bedding and towels for the week.

"It's your vacation," I reminded my ex. "I don't ask you to supply these items for my family trips."

"But it's for the kids," he said.

"You mean *our* kids?" I asked.

Such requests usually come on the cusp of a handover, that time when I volley our children to their father for a visit, and he brings them back a week to ten days later, bags of dirty laundry in tow. As for last summer's beach rental? I stood my ground and refused to supply the three sets of bedding and towels.

One could say I won the battle. Not so for the war. At the end of the trip, I was greeted not only with my children's dirty bed linens, towels, and laundry but with his and his lady friend's dirty bed linens and towels as well. I was advised to store these newly purchased items in my attic should he need them again.

Seriously?

For the upcoming vacation this Saturday, I was already asked to purchase the children's toiletries in advance because he won't have time. Hmmm.

Early on, when I resisted such directives, I was duly warned.

"Just wait and see what you get from me," he once threatened, as though I were a small child who had refused to do her weekly chores.

I reminded him I would get exactly what I was due as per our settlement agreement.

Our exchange reminded me of season nine, episode eight of the '70s sitcom *All in the Family*. The episode, "Edith versus the Bank," begins with Edith deciding to surprise husband Archie with a new color TV for their thirtieth anniversary after theirs breaks. Off-camera, Edith discovers that the department store, and on-camera, the bank won't give her a $500 credit line to buy it because she has no visible assets and doesn't work full time.

When Edith corrects the bank's loan officer about how she does work full time—she does "all the cooking and the cleaning and the washing and the shopping"—he responds, "I mean real work."

"Oh, that's real work," she answers. "Have you ever tried it?"

"That's just housework," the loan officer says.

"What's wrong with housework? Ain't that important?" Edith questions before leaving.

At home, she has no choice but to confront Archie and ask him to lend her the money. When he resists, she says, "Let me ask you something. Do you think that the work I do here in the house—the cooking and the washing and the cleaning and the shopping—is worth a dollar a week?"

"About," Archie concedes.

"Well, I figured it all out," Edith tells him.

And she has. Edith explains to Archie that a dollar a week for thirty years comes to $1,560, meaning he owes money to her, and the loan she's asking for from him wouldn't be a loan at all but, instead, her pay. Back pay.

In the same way, alimony is not a gift from the paying spouse. Its purpose is to compensate the spouse who may unfairly suffer economically as a consequence of divorce. In my case, I stayed home to raise our three children, a decision we made together, forgoing my most valuable earning years.

My ex isn't a bad guy, but sometimes, like Archie, I just don't think he gets it. I am not his wife anymore. When I said, "I do," I meant it. And when I said, "I don't," I meant that too.

I now pass all employee benefits on to his future wife.

In Defense of Gold Diggers: It's Not Always What You Think

When we talk about currency, we talk about the gold standard. When we talk about women who use men for personal gain, we talk about gold diggers. Today, I'm here to talk about another standard—a double one, the one by which men look for women with beaucoup bucks, and the standard by which men rarely get called out for their own parasitic and gold-digging ways.

I rarely write or even speak about money. And there's a reason for that. Although I do have real financial struggles and worries about my future, they are often far removed from those so many other divorced single mothers suffer that to fret about how I will finance my daughters' summer teen tours, son's sleepaway camp, or next family vacation seems, at a minimum, insensitive.

But by the same token, women like myself who are supported almost entirely by the alimony and child support awarded them from their prior marriage do have a problem that goes by largely unnoticed. And that's the inability to consider marrying a man of lesser means, a man who will be unable to support her once she loses that main source of her income.

Before you get all up in arms and start telling me how I should go out and make my own money, please know I'm working on it. Easier said than done. Like so many women, I missed my best earning years while at home raising children. Today,

I'm in my early forties, and although I hold a law degree, I never worked as a lawyer. Opting into an alternative career right after graduation with my husband's guidance and financial support backing me, I knowingly took a pay cut, believing I would one day recoup those losses in a job that I not only loved but in which I also excelled.

One miscarriage later, the subsequent births of three children within five years, a workaholic husband who rarely lent a hand, and a three-year tour living overseas in furtherance of my husband's career goals, I suddenly found myself nearing forty, about to be divorced, faced with full physical custody of my three kids, and no immediate means to support myself and my family on my own.

Unlike so many others, I'm fortunate because my divorce settlement affords me some time. Time to heal my emotional wounds and time to nurture and grow the career I know I was always meant to have. With that said, I wear handcuffs and not the *Fifty Shades of Grey* kind. My handcuffs are golden, and they prevent me, to a large extent, from dating men whose earnings will not allow me to consider leaving the security I presently have, the security I earned by forgoing a potentially lucrative career to stay home and raise my children while my then-husband built his own.

Currently, I'm being compensated for the opportunity cost of working as a stay-at-home mom, a decision my husband and I made together, and for the privilege that I have today of raising three children almost entirely by myself.

From a financial perspective, my decision to date only successful men makes perfect fiscal sense. By every calculation, the numbers support it. However, from the standpoint of finding everlasting love, it limits my choices and forces me to confront a theorem that on its face appears not only cold and shallow but is difficult to prove as well. That's because our culture tells us love conquers all.

But does it really?

At first glance, many may dismiss me as a gold digger. But that's not the case. What I truly seek is love and a deep connection with a lifelong partner, not expensive dinners and gifts. But the realities of my situation, my current inability to support my children and myself without spousal support, force me to consider the financial stability of the men who contend for that role in my life.

When I ask a man what exactly it is that he does for a living, it's not because I'm looking for someone to shake down for a new designer bag or a lavish vacation. I can make those purchases on my own should that be the way I decide to prioritize my spending, which it's not. The "toys" I sport—jewelry, handbags, and a sizable wardrobe—are remnants of a former life, a life in which I was given gifts instead of the love and intimacy I desired.

Yet somehow when I show up to a date, I'm often met with financial questions that, if I should be the one to ask them, would immediately place me in the category of gold digger. Questions including: How do you support yourself? Did you get your house in the divorce? Is your watch a Cartier? How many square feet is your home? What kind of car do you drive? Do you own or lease your SUV? Who designed your bag, sweater, or boots? The list goes on.

Are these guys digging for gold? Maybe yes. Maybe no. Early on, I have no way of determining that. But the bottom line is men have as much at stake in knowing what they are potentially getting into as women do. Fair enough. I need to be privy to such information myself.

The trouble is when this line of questioning comes from a man, it's not perceived as gold digging but, rather, due diligence, good business acumen, and a sign of his intelligence.

I call bullshit.

I would like nothing more than to meet some hunky contractor who not only can rock my world but who can do home repairs as well. What a little slice of heaven on Earth that would be. Or a middle-management executive who leaves work at a reasonable hour, doesn't need to travel for his job, and isn't always attached to his phone. But right now, that's simply not a risk I can afford to take.

It's not that I want what's yours. It's that I don't know if I can give up what's mine.

The 'Clueless' Ways Women Try to Manipulate Men—and Why They Fail

About a month ago, I had dinner with a guy I used to see. We soon began exchanging dating stories, one of my favorite conversation topics. I must admit I'm always fascinated by how other women behave with men. So when he told me about a woman he recently dated who began acting "crazy," I was all ears.

According to my friend, they had seen each other only twice and, after the second date, he didn't follow up with her again. But instead of reaching out to him and saying hi to see where they stood, this forty-something-year-old woman instead decided on a less direct and, let's just say, more creative approach.

As my friend recalled the text the woman "accidentally" sent to him, I became suspicious. In it, she described, clearly to someone else, her irritation with my friend for not contacting her again.

"Did you respond?" I asked, trying to mask the smirk that was already forming around my mouth.

"No," he replied, shrugging his shoulders. "I assumed it was sent to me by mistake."

Yeah, there was a mistake, all right. But it wasn't hers. It was his, though he had absolutely no idea how he had blundered.

"So what happened next?" I inquired as if I didn't know the answer, which, of course, I already did.

"She began sending me angry texts about how it must be over between us."

He still had absolutely no idea why she was so upset.

"Don't you get it?" I pressed.

My friend, a successful, Ivy League-educated, high-level executive, stared at me. "No, I don't."

"Silly man," I explained. "You failed her test. When she sent you that text, she was trying to goad you into reaching out to her. When you didn't respond, that's when she lost it."

He stared at me in disbelief. "That's so manipulative."

No shit, Sherlock.

My friend learned something new that evening, which was how some women use manipulative tactics to get what they want, in this case, a text intended for someone else, or so she wanted him to think, that said everything she wanted to say to him directly but chose not to. But I believe it's really the women who pull this kind of crap (you know who you are) who have something to learn here.

As can be seen from this example, though informative of her disappointment with the relationship's progression, the text did absolutely nothing to inspire him to act in the manner she wanted. Instead, he took the text at face value (as men usually do because, well, they're not women), assumed it wasn't directed at him, and likely never gave it a second thought until our conversation that night. In other words, he still did what he wanted to do. Or didn't want to do, which was call her. When she became enraged, my friend received confirmation that he had indeed made the right decision to end things, which was the opposite of what the woman was trying to achieve in the first place.

Uncommon behavior? Hardly. I hear stories like this all the time. And in each and every scenario, the guy remains clueless to the mind games women play or the smoke signals they send, especially when there's no fire.

Which reminds me of yet another smart and successful guy I know who, like my other friend, received multiple texts from the same woman that were clearly meant for someone else. Or so he believed.

"She must be stupid," he stated, knowing no other way to explain the frequent errors.

"What do the texts say?" I asked, already anticipating the inventive attention grabber I knew I was about to hear.

"Stop coming to my office" and "Stop sending me gifts," he repeated with a straight face.

I smiled. It was apparent, to me at least, the texts were intended to make him jealous that another guy (likely by the name of George Glass) was interested in her. Yet he remained clueless nonetheless.

You might be wondering right now whether her efforts paid off. It seems not since today he remains unattached.

But the most ridiculous story that I've heard was told to me only the other morning. One of my friend's female co-workers snapped a picture of flowers sent to someone else at work.

The woman then texted the photo to her own boyfriend, asking whether or not he had sent the flowers to her since they arrived without a card which, of course, they didn't. His answer? A simple and resounding . . . no. Suffice it to say that as of this writing, she has yet to receive any "surprise" deliveries from her beau.

The mastermind behind this last antic took a page right out of Cher Horowitz's playbook in the 1995 hit movie *Clueless*. In the film, Cher, portrayed by Alicia Silverstone, goes as far as to send herself flowers at school in order to attract the attention of Christian, her handsome gentleman classmate. True to form, Cher fared about as well as the woman above did, although for different reasons, and her ruse failed in the end.

But I wonder, if the efforts of these women were successful, would either of them have wanted those flowers anyway, under such questionable circumstances? I know I wouldn't. In fact, I'm hard-pressed to understand why any woman would want a guy to send her flowers, ask her out, or shower her with gifts if she has to, however subtly, twist his arm. More likely than not, if a guy does do what a woman hints at, his attention will be short-lived regardless because the overtures aren't genuine to begin with.

The man who will win your heart will win it because he wants to win it. He will make his affection known to you and, because of that, there will be no doubt in your mind as to his feelings. So if you find yourself questioning your guy's behavior and then scheming how best to call him to action because you believe he doesn't know the way, understand it's not he who is clueless. It's you.

Straight from a Guy: How to Let Him Down Easy

I was recently out for a drink with a guy when we began trading dating horror stories. This is usually my favorite part of a first date because I always manage to be amused while still learning something new.

That night was no exception. This particular guy, who was in his mid-forties and never married, gave me his "list" of deal breakers about ten minutes after meeting, at which point for me, the date magically transitioned from a date into what I like to call "research."

First, he said a woman must not wear too much perfume. OK, I can appreciate that. No one likes to be stifled with a fragrance to the point where they can't taste their food. Second, a woman must not go to the bathroom in front of him. Bummer, I was saving that for the second date. Third, a woman must not burp in his face. Who the hell has this guy been seeing?

The list went on from there with no improvement. She must not have bad breath; she must not be cheap; she must earn her own money; and, if applicable, she must not spend too much time calling to check on her kids during a date. Judging by his comments, it was apparent that he was looking for someone very special.

What I didn't do was reciprocate by giving him my list, which happens to include guys who have lists and guys like him who, as he admitted, sometimes book three dates back-to-back in the same evening. Instead, I countered with a story about a guy I went out with three times who kept asking me out even though I let him know I was no longer interested in seeing him.

"Well, what did you say?" my date asked smugly.

"I kept telling him I was busy," I said, proud of my capacity for politeness.

My date shook his head with knowing disapproval. He said women do this all the time and are then surprised the guy keeps coming back with alternatives.

"You need to tell a guy you like him like a brother," he advised matter-of-factly.

Huh? Then I thought about it. It actually sounded like valuable dating advice in its apparent stupidity, ahem, simplicity. That statement would be a safe way to put the kibosh on any chance of a guy thinking we were moving forward.

When the date was finally over, and the cosmopolitan I was nursing had successfully taken the edge off my thoughts of "How did this become my life?" he gave me a quick hug good-bye and asked if I would be OK walking alone to my car. Sure, what's a little black ice on the sidewalk and a dark parking lot?

When the phone rang a day and a half later, I was surprised. He wanted to see me again! I assume my breath must have been passable, and I sufficiently neglected my three kids at home during our date.

I know my comments may sound snide, but I really am a nice person, and I don't like to say no. So I thought no but said yes anyway. Damn, I've got to stop doing this.

But the truth is I know he's not my guy, and I don't want to lead him to believe that he is. I also don't want to worry about having to kiss him goodnight, which I already have been for the past three days. Definitely a bad sign.

I've changed a lot in the time since my separation. I'm much clearer now about what I want and what I don't. And I'm happy to say, these days, I'm content waiting for the right person instead of forcing relationships that shouldn't be.

So when we speak tonight, I'm going to tell him the truth. I'm going to tell him I like him like a brother.

I only wonder if he'll appreciate the irony.

Playing the Single Mom Card

As I stepped out of the car onto the curb at Newark Airport last Saturday to embark on a four-night trip to Austin, I breathed a heavy sigh of relief that I successfully made it out the door. The preparation leading up to my departure had been harried as usual. As a single mom, I must get a lot of ducks in a row to enjoy a long weekend on my own, not as someone's mom or, as in the past, someone's wife, but as me, the woman I'm getting to know. I smiled to myself. I was tired but satisfied. Content at the moment. Excited for the days ahead.

I made my way through the airport, pretty sure I hadn't forgotten anything and not really caring if I did. When I reached security, I got in line with all the excited families leaving for winter break, destined for fun in the sun or hot chocolate-filled ski trips. My own family, now fragmented and broken as a consequence of my recent divorce, would be separated this school vacation, my children leaving the next day with their dad for the Bahamas. I was, it seemed, the only lone traveler in a sea of happy families.

I could practically taste the non-fat latte that called to me from Starbucks on the other side of security when an airport employee ordered me off the line, pronto.

"Do you see the sign?" he hollered, causing heads to turn, expressionless in their complacency. "You're only allowed to have two carry-on bags. You have three."

"I have one carry-on bag, a computer, and my handbag," I explained. "I've never had a problem traveling with these items before."

"Get. Off. The. Line." His voice got louder with every utterance.

I glanced down at my watch. The airport was crowded, still regrouping from yet another snowstorm two days earlier, the umpteenth one that plagued the Northeast this winter. Coupled with the crowds traveling for winter break, I knew I didn't have a lot of cushion time before I would come dangerously close to missing my flight.

"I'm traveling alone," I pleaded. "What am I supposed to do?"

"That's your problem," he sneered.

I stood silent, watching the crowds of people file through security, many carrying the same items as I was. Of course it was my problem. It was always my problem. I was alone, and I felt it.

My eyes welled with tears.

Another airport employee nearby, witnessing the commotion, questioned her co-worker why I was being singled out. She looked quizzical.

"Please," I said to her. "I'm here by myself." I have no one to take my computer, and I need to have it with me. Please."

Then, to my surprise, I said it. Out loud, for the world to hear. To judge.

"I'm a single mom."

I was mortified. I had just asked for special treatment because I'm raising kids alone. Kids who weren't even with me. I cringed as I heard the words escape me. Had I just implied I have a disability of some sort? Did I subconsciously believe I was deserving of special treatment because I have no husband? I felt like a disgrace to women everywhere.

The two co-workers began arguing. Minutes later, and to the original airport employee's chagrin, he aborted his attack and allowed me back in line. I thanked the female employee for her assistance and went on my way, trying to make sense of the implication of my words.

My life as a single mom is challenging, more challenging than it ever was when I was married, even to a workaholic husband who was rarely home to help. In addition to the monetary, physical, and logistical challenges, the emotional impact of raising three children alone is something I struggle with every single day. It never leaves me, even when the children are thousands of miles from my side.

As I thought about it, I realized I didn't utter those words in shame. I stated them with pride. I'm a single mom. I've come this far and am still going further. Never will I stay silent while someone singles me out because I'm alone.

No, I didn't have time for my morning coffee. But I made my flight. The irony is I wasn't playing the single mom card that morning.

I was living it.

The Day My Ex Thought I Was 'Taken,' and What I Was Given Back

Stories aren't told. They tell themselves. In their own time. When they're ready to be revealed and ready to be heard. When their meaning can be ascribed to something other than a stroke of bad luck or poor judgment. When we know why that story has become embedded in the fabric of our lives.

"You must write about this," the woman across the table from me urged.

I had minutes ago finished recounting to her—another divorcée traveling through Eastern Europe with her two college-aged children and a complete stranger to me—how I came to eat dinner with them alone on my second and last night in Munich.

"No," I replied. "I wouldn't know what to say."

"You will," she assured. "You will."

In a small touristy restaurant that paired strangers at communal tables, I dined on wiener schnitzel and apple strudel in the presence of waitstaff dressed in traditional German garb for over-emphasized dramatic effect. I couldn't help but smile at the room's traditional but tired décor as it evoked happy memories of the family vacations I spent in Epcot with my then young and complete family.

I missed being part of a couple but no longer missed the man I had been coupled with for nearly a quarter of a century. Newly divorced, I struggled with little success that evening and for many evenings to come to make sense of the turn of events that brought me to that dinner table, separated by thousands of miles of ocean from my three children, without anyone by my side.

Those days make perfect sense to me now.

During that last ride on the dating merry-go-round since separating, I had finally grabbed for and believed I captured the brass ring—my dignity. My convictions were finally my own; a feat recently accomplished as I closed the door for what I believed the last time on a demeaning non-relationship relationship. I knew I wanted more. And, after unrelenting heartache, I finally believed I deserved more.

It should have been a time of accomplishment and pride. I had defined my boundaries, no longer agreeing to compromise my values and my morals in the hopes of finding true love. Yet there I was again, licking my wounds from another kick from a universe that never seemed to reward me for maintaining my self-respect.

My family and close friends had begged me not to go. And I had seriously thought about not going—but for all the wrong reasons. Which, of course, led me to the wrong decision, one that left me isolated and vulnerable in a foreign city I had never before visited less than an hour after reconnecting with the man I was there to see. As I read the proverbial writing on the wall, I called my ex-husband for urgent help.

"I'm in trouble," was all I needed to say.

Without hesitation or question, he obliged. With one quick instruction to his personal assistant, my ex-husband, like Liam Neeson's character Bryan Mills did for his daughter in the 2008 film *Taken*, plucked me from a situation in which my naïveté had caused me to become entangled. Thanks to his accessible resources and a quick swipe of his credit card, I had been rescued.

And defeated.

Before leaving on that fateful trip, I had enjoyed two dates with someone new, a third penned on the calendar. My mother suggested I cancel my pre-arranged trip in part because of this new prospect, but more so because I would be traveling with someone whom I knew only a couple of months and not all that well. In light of her ardent protests, I considered it but not enough.

In my mind, canceling equated to hedging my bet, deciding which potential relationship was more promising, and choosing between the two. Of course, there was never a choice in my mind. It was always the second of the two—the man who espoused the same values I did, the man with more of a similar background to mine, the man who was more local, and the man I was actually interested in seeing again. The man I did end up seeing again for nearly five months.

But when he announced on our second date his recent registration with an online dating service sometime between our first and second dates and revealed that he had dated different women almost every night over the course of the previous week, my decision became obvious. The late Maya Angelou summed it up best when she said, "Never make someone a priority when all you are to them is an option."

So I didn't.

By all accounts, it's healthy advice. Yet somehow, I was misdirected by it. And though I was an option to both men as they were to me, I failed to make myself a priority in either scenario. I rested my decision on where I would receive the most attention, not on what was best for me.

Up in my newly reserved room, in a cold, commercial American-owned hotel that stood out in stark contrast to the centuries-old streetscape, an inviting morning sun streamed through my window. Feeling like an unwelcome guest, I pulled the curtains closed and crawled into bed instead, sick from the near-bronchitis I had been nursing over the previous few days and jet-lagged from the nine-hour flight plus three hours spent on the ground in Munich International Airport, where I had waited without word from the man I was meeting that his flight had been delayed. No warning of his late arrival, no arrangement made for my retrieval, no address provided for the friend's home where we would be staying so I could, at a minimum, travel there earlier myself. Just silence, leaving me only with a void where I could place my mounting trepidation.

The itinerary had been set a couple of weeks earlier. We were to meet in Munich, spending one night in a home his local friend and business associate shared with his long-time girlfriend before traveling with our hosts to Prague for an extended weekend. Another woman from my gentleman friend's hometown, traveling through Europe alone, was to join us the first night of our stay.

I questioned the sleeping arrangements and was reassured if space were tight, he and I would stay elsewhere. This woman was scheduled to depart the next day anyway, and he seemed

122

pleased with the limited overlap of her visit, citing her tendency to become irritating to him the more time they spent together. Though not entirely comfortable, even after his reassurances, I agreed anyway.

Only days before my trip, the man I was scheduled to meet informed me he had invited this same female friend to extend her stay and join in on the weekend to Prague. After thinking it over, I voiced my discomfort and offered to cancel my trip altogether so as not to deprive him of this weekend excursion. He insisted I still come, offering to stay back in Munich at the friend's home with me while they traveled. Ignoring my uneasiness for the second time, I again decided to move forward with my plans.

Nearly three hours after I had landed, my gentleman friend's flight arrived, and he retrieved me from the airport restaurant where I had been sitting. We then met up at baggage claim with our host, who was waiting to drive us to his Munich home. But in a matter of moments, our host started pressuring me to leave with them for Prague within the hour. My gentleman friend didn't intervene despite our agreed-upon arrangement.

I was angry, having just flown all that way to see him. Which is why sometime during the twenty-minute ride to our destination, I made a flippant offer to stay behind in Munich while he went on to Prague for the weekend without me, an offer he jumped at and accepted by the time we parked.

At that point, I knew what I had to do.

Within minutes of my arrival at our host's apartment, and after the phone call to my ex-husband, I picked up my bag and walked straight out the door. My gentleman friend not only let me go, but he also picked up the back end of my duffel bag in silence as I dragged it down four flights of stairs and dropped it on the street before turning his back and walking away without a word.

For months, I have carried this shame. Shame because I can't blame anyone for this debacle except myself. I should have known better. Or should I have?

I retold this story recently while on yet another first date. When I finished, my date, without judgment, asked, "Do you know what a mulligan is?"

I didn't. I looked back at him, wide-eyed with confusion.

A mulligan, he explained, is a golfing term used to describe a second chance given to a player following a blunder. My trip, synonymous with yet another misguided attempt at finding a healthy relationship, was just that—and one (if not many) to which we're all entitled.

Yes, I had swung—badly—and missed. But that swing was no different from those other bad swings before it, and not any that would come after. Except with one notable difference: with each subsequent swing, my stroke continues to improve.

A failed marriage is the same. Divorce is its mulligan, the mulligan affording each of us a second chance to get back what we lost and discover what we have not yet had. I, for one, still plan on taking that chance because, as the legendary golfer Ben Hogan once said, "The most important shot in golf is the next one."

How Thinking Like a Man Helped Me Begin Thinking Like a Woman

"You have daughters."

That's what I said to him. Actually, it was more like "You. Have. Daughters." As in, "What the hell are you doing treating a woman (me!) like *this*?!?!"

It was one of the quickest relationships in the history of relationships, I'm sure. Why? Because I'm finally, *finally* (thank you, God) thinking like a man. And though that makes me savvy, even smart, it also makes me sad. Sad that I must think this way to protect myself and sad that I'm beginning to no longer believe that there's a man out there who will ever see me as anything beyond something (not even someone) to fuck.

Yeah, today's the day. Today I'm calling it like it is or, I should say, how I see it. I'm sick of the damaged guys. The ones whose ex-wives are a bunch of "cunts" or "bitches" (their words) who took half of their savings, their house, years of alimony and child support, their kids, and whatever else they could get their grubby hands on. Those women who, according to their exes, never worked, slept all day, and were, at best, mediocre mothers.

In fairness, women aren't any better. Tales of husbands who worked around the clock, neglected their wives, and took the kids away from Mommy, stepping on her toes as they did.

Sadly, these stories are as much truth as they are lies. And we, the outsiders, the "date," will likely never know which are which.

But we believe anyway. We trust the guys. We may say we don't. But we do. And it's not because we have to but because we want to. We want so badly to believe that this guy will be different from all the rest before him. We want to believe that this guy is the guy looking for the whole woman, not only a body to keep him warm for a night.

Now, back to the guy. Our date was, by all accounts, a good one. Stimulating conversation. Chemistry. Not off-the-charts chemistry (I've experienced that before, and this wasn't it), but more than enough to keep me interested and more than enough to move beyond a first date.

So when our Sunday six-and-a-half-hour date neared the end, after kisses were exchanged beginning midway through dinner, he asked what I was doing the rest of the week because he would love to have me to his house and cook me dinner.

Loved the idea, only not for a second date. However, I didn't flat out reject the concept, wanting instead time to think it over.

We threw around our parenting schedules. Between the two of us, the only nights that worked were Monday night (the next night and less than twenty-four hours later) and Wednesday night. Otherwise, we would have to wait until the following week, which was fine with me. After all, what was the rush?

Monday is always a crazy day for me, and I told him so. Besides that, I told him it was too soon. "Don't you want time to . . . digest?" I asked. He laughed, though I'm not convinced he agreed.

Tuesday was off the table for me as well because of a previously scheduled commitment. Wednesday, though not great either, was a possibility, and I left off that I would try to arrange a ride home for my daughter from her evening activity.

He texted me late that night after our date to make sure I made it home and again the next day. After we exchanged texts, he called. Called! Loved this guy. He was doing everything right. In fact, we had already spoken on the phone several times before our first date, indicating to me he preferred calling to texting. Yes!

But when he called me Monday night, one day since we saw each other, it somehow went to hell within minutes.

We asked about each other's days. Exchanged some tidbits. And then he asked whether Wednesday would work for dinner. I told him that a weeknight would be tricky, even with a ride for my daughter. He lived about an hour and a half away, and though I didn't mind driving (I actually love to drive), it would be during rush hour, and I had to wake up early the next morning. But not wanting the same plan rescheduled for the following week, I mentioned that I was also uncomfortable with the venue for a second date.

He laughed and said he understood but then added that he doesn't like "doing dinner" over and over again. Agreed. Nothing is worse than the never-ending string of dinners kind of relationship, the relationship where there's never a night of take-out and movie watching, a lazy Sunday reading the newspaper and watching football, or an impromptu night during the week of mind-blowing sex and a sleepover. But we only had one date, and those other plans come with time.

As I was about to suggest an alternative, something in between a long, drawn-out dinner out and an intimate meal for which I was not yet ready, the phone cut out. Not an uncommon phenomenon in my house, and I assumed the problem was on my end. I called back and went straight to voicemail. Perhaps he was trying me at the same time? I thought I'd better wait. But when he didn't call me within the next few minutes, I tried two more times and got the same result. I sent a text telling him the call had dropped and that my calls kept going to voicemail. Then, I waited.

The minutes passed. But my phone never rang. I was incredulous. Was it actually as it seemed? Had he really lost interest because I nixed dinner at his house?

"Please," I thought, "let me be wrong."

I'm not the type of woman who calls after a guy blows her off to ask what happened, to find out why he disappeared. The very fact that he did has always been a sufficient enough reason for me never to speak to him again. I've done it to others. Though rejection never feels good, I know whatever I say isn't going to change anyone's mind, nor would I want it to.

But that night, I made an exception. Not because I wanted anything from him. He was already done in my eyes. But I wanted him to know that I knew.

Thirty minutes later, when I knew it was clear I had been blown off, I picked up the phone.

"Are you really that guy?" I asked, calm, poised, cool.

Because I know that guy. I dated that guy, though I never said so on the phone. That guy was more than a little perturbed that I wasn't ready for an intimate night on our last-minute Fourth of July second date. According to him, every restaurant in the area was closed for the holiday. So cooking for me in his house would be the only option. Say what? When I reiterated that I wasn't comfortable with this arrangement, he found a local restaurant that was open (surprise!) and proceeded to spit nails through the entire meal, after which I never heard from him again.

Good call on the candlelight dinner, I guess. Better than a candlelight vigil the day after, waiting for a call that would never come.

It's important to note that just because a woman and a man have dinner together in either her home or his doesn't automatically mean sex is the final course. But being in such an intimate setting and close proximity to a bedroom can make for an uncomfortable situation or one in which events simply get out of hand before either the man or woman wants them to.

My new friend laughed at my insinuation. He explained that his phone had died for no apparent reason. It was obvious it was working again since he was on it, but still, he hadn't bothered to call back. At a minimum, it made him rude.

What I should have assumed, according to him, was that something horrible had happened, and that's why he went MIA. Yes, he said this, and then I was the one who was laughing, though I found little about this exchange funny.

I listened and afterward explained how the situation appeared from my perspective and that leaving our plans up in the air had left me feeling miffed. Then I said goodnight, knowing full well I would never hear from him again.

And that was fine with me. Because by the time I put down the phone, I realized I had been mistaken. No, I wasn't thinking like a man, whatever that may be. Not even close. I was thinking like a woman who values herself. Like a woman who loves herself.

It took me a while, if not my entire lifetime, to get here. And I'm not going anywhere I don't want to be.

'Crazy, Stupid, Love,' and STIs. You Have Every Right to Worry.

Last winter, I began experiencing shortness of breath and a burning sensation when I inhaled. I went to see a pulmonologist who confirmed I was not, in fact, suffering from lung cancer (as I had so convinced myself) but, instead, acid reflux. He prescribed a regimen I never followed, a decision that landed me back in my GP's office last week, this time convinced I was dying.

My doctor wasn't buying it and suggested I "speak to someone" about how to better cope with my anxiety. I wasn't buying that either and asked him to order a panel of blood work to prove me wrong. Then, like the responsible, sexually active divorced woman I am, I asked him to throw in an HIV test for good measure.

A couple of days later, I called my doctor's office to get the results. According to the nurse, she couldn't give me them over the phone because the doctor hadn't read the report yet. But being the hypochondriac I am, I suspected from the tone of her voice (in reality, there was no tone) that she was lying, that she could see the results (even though she said she couldn't), and knew for sure I was doomed.

But I played it cool and agreed to wait for her call. When I hadn't heard back from her by the end of the day, I called the office again. This time, the nurse requested I hold for the doctor.

"That's it," I thought. "I'm finished." Doctors only get on the phone to deliver bad news.

My mind raced. I had ignored the signs for months, the nondescript symptoms, and now my luck was about to run out. What would it be? Esophageal cancer? Stomach cancer? Ovarian cancer?

Then it hit me. "Wait a second. No . . . It can't be. Maybe I have . . ."

I thought back to the guy I had been on and off with for years. And that once faithful but soon-to-be ex-husband I had dated for a while whose wife had cheated on him. Then to my ex-husband, who had cheated on me.

My runaway train of thought was broken when my doctor picked up the phone. With a quick hello, he began rattling off my results, spewing medical gibberish I couldn't possibly comprehend nor wanted to.

"What about my HIV test?" I interrupted, abandoning for the moment my cancer fears.

"I'll get to that in a minute." He was cryptic. At least I imagined he was.

He really wasn't. As it turned out, he was reading the report for the first time with me on the phone and reading it in order, no less.

But he wasn't getting it. Getting me. What he failed to appreciate was that I needed to find out how this chapter would end before I would allow him to read it to me.

So I interrupted again, this time more forcefully.

"Do you have my HIV results?" I said, my voice becoming more high-pitched with every syllable.

He paused, probably because he was looking for the information I demanded. Instead, I imagined him taking the time he needed to compose himself before giving me the bad news.

"You're negative," he finally replied. "Can I continue now?"

"Sure," I said. "But you need to start from the beginning since I didn't hear a word you said."

My doctor laughed. I laughed. We laughed together.

Until he let me in on what he was really thinking: "The reason you're so worried about HIV is that you're not being completely honest with me about your sexual history."

I stopped laughing.

Huh?

Not being honest with . . . him? What, were he and I now dating or something?

At first, I was defensive.

Then I thought about it. My sexual history is altogether irrelevant. That's because it only takes one.

My doctor assured me I was healthy. At least physically.

In fact, at that moment, I never felt healthier, especially after having gotten so fired up that I nearly forgot why I had come to see him in the first place.

There I was, being cautious. Responsible. And suddenly feeling slut-shamed as a consequence.

My doctor claimed he was only joking. Only I didn't think he was very funny.

Safe sex (really safer sex) is no laughing matter. Contracting an STI is something I do worry about. Something we all should worry about, especially as many of us get back on the proverbial horse after leaving the presumed safety of our marriages behind. Recently separated Cal Weaver, played by Steve Carell, summed it up best in the 2011 film *Crazy, Stupid, Love* when he said, "I'm a little worried you have AIDS" to his first "hookup" post-separation. The scene, meant to be funny, does hit home.

There is one thing my doctor does have a right to be concerned about: I do need to take my stress level down a notch. I'll give him that.

Except not when it comes to my sexual health. About that, I will remain vigilant.

So to you, dear doctor, and anyone else who implies to a woman that her being concerned about STIs points to her promiscuity, I say, "Go fuck yourself."

All I ask is that you practice safe sex when you do.

Does Lust Know No Bounds? Is Age Only a Number?

I'm done. Finished. Kaput. Had it. No more looking for a new father for my kids, as the stereotype about single moms has me doing. I'm totally over it. Finito. That's because I've finally discovered something more worthwhile to pursue for them—a new grandfather.

Yep. That's right. This past week, I decided I'm officially going all Anna Nicole Smith on my ass and looking for a mature man. (Actually, they come looking for me, but that's beside the point.) One who can construct a sentence that doesn't begin with "Hey, beautiful" and ends with me blocking him from all contact. A man I can lean on when I need to, a man who will make all that ails me disappear by suggesting something other than his magic wand to do it.

I've dated older men before and liked it. There's something to be said for a man who remembers what it's like to date. To court. Who understands exactly what a date is. Who doesn't ask me to chill, hook up, hang out, connect (Is that literal?), or meet up. Is that too much to ask? I may read *Elite Daily*, but I'm in no way its target audience. So why the hell am I so easily able to relate?

Houston, we have a problem.

That's why when I received a well-written email from a more "mature" man on Jdate, I was intrigued. Though he had no photo (a big no-no for me), I emailed him back and requested one. He sent me five, each with a description so I could get a general sense of him.

He had a bit of a Kris Kringle thing going on but without the Santa physique. So maybe more like a Colonel Sanders type. No, I'm just kidding. Sort of. But I'm not a fan of a lot of facial hair, so what he was sporting would definitely have to go. I agreed to speak while reserving my right not to pursue anything further based on his age of sixty-one, with which I wasn't all that comfortable.

During our conversation, he told me that he split time between his various homes, spending most of the year at his island house.

"You mean like Richard Branson?" I joked. But he wasn't kidding, as I saw from the aerial shot he later provided of his mansion situated on a private island smack in the middle of a picturesque lake.

"Hell," I thought, "I can be the Ginger to his Professor." But that image quickly turned to one of me running through the jungle in *Lord of the Flies*, and I imagined yet another call to my ex-husband, this time to the tune of: "I'm in trouble again. I need you to send a helicopter ASAP."

We spoke on the phone for over an hour, most of the conversation spent with me educating him on today's dating etiquette or lack thereof. Apparently, I didn't do a very good job because he wanted to speak the next night again, ad nauseam.

"No can do, buddy," was the general crux of my next email. I told him I would be shuffling my kids (perhaps his future grandkids) back and forth to evening activities in between working. In actuality, I spent the last part of the night reading a book, happily enjoying the solitude. Was I emotionally unavailable or just not that into him? I wasn't sure.

As the week wore on, I became ambivalent if not unenthused about our upcoming date while he, I would later learn, got a haircut (hope he didn't shave on my account) and purchased a small gift for me.

Gift?

Reminded me of that scene in *Must Love Dogs* when Sarah Nolan, played by Diane Lane, shows up to a blind date she was unaware she made with her father after reading the personal ads. In the film, he greets her with a single yellow rose. Yuck. A gift on a first date for me is when a guy doesn't squeeze my ass or try to slide his hand up my dress. Done and done.

When he didn't hear from me again the next day, he sent me yet another email asking to make our date—museum and dinner—even earlier.

Honestly, I couldn't go through with it. And it didn't have anything at all to do with his age. Because if one sixty-two-year-old Liam Neeson were asking, I would be there in a heartbeat. He can "take" me any day.

My canceling had everything to do with attraction, from his photo to his voice to our conversation to . . . whatever else didn't float my boat, except the year in which he was born, notwithstanding he had a boat. And probably a nice one at that.

Though my mother was relieved, I did feel bad. I was to be his first date in decades, and he was disappointed. When I responded to his email about the time change, I wished him well, to which he sent me what amounted to a 500-word love letter.

Yep, last week I found myself auditioning to be step-mama to a guy's six-year-old who he insisted on introducing me to during our third and what became our final date, and this week, for a starring role in *The Notebook*, part three.

Didn't this guy hear? Nicholas Sparks is getting divorced, and everyone is saying love is officially dead. I can only imagine that last letter Nicholas sent to his wife, Cathy:

Dearest Cathy,

You keep the house in New Bern, and I'll take the one on the Outer Banks. I hear chicks really dig it out there . . .

Love may be dead, but lust isn't. And I, for one, need both.

Liam, I'm ready if you are.

The Important Dating Tip I Learned from Mister Rogers

When I was in preschool, I loved watching Mister Rogers' Neighborhood. My mother still laughs whenever she reminds me how I used to wave to strangers in the supermarket, yelling, "Hi, Neighbor!" at the top of my lungs.

As each episode concluded, Mister Rogers always sang the goodbye song, "It's Such a Good Feeling," removed his cardigan, put on his jacket, and promised to return the next day. In doing so, he taught all of us that goodbyes are important and bring a "very good feeling" to others. The lesson seems straightforward.

Why then do so many relationships end without a proper goodbye?

From an isolated date to a committed relationship, from a casual relationship to marriage, stories in which one person disappears without a word or with such a brief explanation as to leave the jilted party dumbfounded are commonplace. Here one minute, gone the next. Up in smoke. The effect can be frustrating, maddening even, and altogether devastating.

Gratuitous phrases used as feeble attempts to tidy up the messiness of a failed relationship, succinct statements such as "Good luck to you" or "I wish you all the best," can actually be more damaging than helpful. The curtness of these statements, the coldness with which they are offered, often do not measure up against the length or depth of the relationship, leaving burning questions unanswered and the blindsided party left wondering what went wrong. As the goodbye song describes, the "things you want to talk about" are inevitably ignored, and a proper goodbye ultimately falls by the wayside.

Equally upsetting is leaving someone with the promise of a call or to see each other soon and then not making good on that promise. Again, the same questions are left unanswered, but this time, the aggrieved party does not even benefit from the platitude or the façade that the other person cared even the slightest bit.

All day long, I say goodbye to people. Whether it is a friend I meet for lunch, some random stranger I converse with while waiting in line at the bank, or the exterminator who calls to remind me of my upcoming quarterly service, I bring some sort of closure to our interaction. At a minimum, it is a show of respect. I am letting the other person know that, for the time we were dealing with one another, what he or she said mattered.

For the time being or forever, saying goodbye in a platonic relationship is arguably a less emotionally charged process. When it comes to matters of the heart, the situation is not always as easy to navigate. I admit that it is simpler to turn the other way while the jilted person visibly suffers. That way, we do not have to look into someone else's eyes and see the pain we have inflicted.

I cannot claim to have always been tolerant of someone else's feelings. When I first began dating after my separation, I went out on three dates with a very nice guy. By the third date, however, I no longer wanted to continue seeing him. When he kept attempting to make plans with me, instead of being honest with him about my feelings, I avoided him and, I hate to say it, disappeared. He was, to say the least, angry, and I was the recipient of a slew of nasty texts and emails telling me so.

I know my handling of the situation was unkind. He was a nice person and was nice to me. I should have come clean and perhaps even acknowledged a specific quality I liked about him, but regrettably, I still did not think we were right for each other in the long run.

In the end, only we can give ourselves the closure we crave. But how much easier would it be for our former romantic interest to achieve that sense of closure if we simply finished things off properly? No one wants to feel the sting of rejection, and we should take some responsibility for the pain our decision causes another. Karma is a bitch, and the likelihood of standing on either side of the rejection fence is real.

It is important to remember that exiting a romantic interaction with dignity also spares someone else's dignity in the process. We all want to come away knowing that we mattered. That the kiss we once shared was, even for a fleeting moment, meaningful. That the knowing glance we exchanged will be remembered. That the passion we shared was heartfelt. That the long conversations we spent exposing our vulnerabilities will be held sacred.

To up and leave a relationship or, even worse, disappear and not show respect for the other person, we insult them by devaluing the time we spent together. And that, as Mister Rogers would likely argue, is not a very good feeling at all.

How I Got My Groove Back

I haven't been feeling right lately. Definitely haven't been myself. At first, my symptoms were nondescript. Lethargy. Apathy. Then I developed this awful taste in my mouth. The onset of my symptoms most often occurred when I turned on the computer, when I saw those smiling pictures staring back at me. Calling out to me. All those "easy-going" guys, the guys who have "a great sense of humor," and the "hopeless romantics" who enjoy Broadway shows and long walks on the beach at sunset.

After some research, I was relieved to learn my illness isn't uncommon for people like me, people who are single and find dates online. Online Dating Fatigue (ODF) is the clinical name of what ails me. And thankfully, there's a cure.

According to experts, the course of treatment is simple. Turn off the computer, take a break from cyberspace, and get out into the real world to meet some real people in person. And that's exactly what I did last Sunday. On that day, I woke up a little earlier, spent an hour on the treadmill, a half-hour in the bathtub, put on my dancing shoes (or boots, in this case), and went to a line dancing class through a Meetup group for Jewish singles ages thirty-five to fifty.

I've gone to Meetup events before, but only ones held in a Manhattan bar setting. And never with any success. I'm not really a "meet market" (or the more pejorative "meat market") kind of girl. Standing at contrived social functions tends to make me uncomfortable. So as a compromise, I found an activity I would like to participate in, where I could also learn something.

Once I saw the venue, a small neighborhood synagogue a few towns away, I realized my efforts might have been misguided. Inside, I was transported back to the 1960s, the time the building appeared to have last been refurbished. When I signed in and paid my five dollars for the registration fee, I was informed the group was not as advertised but, instead, an assortment of men and women ages fifty and up. Way up. But I reminded myself I was there for a dual purpose. I was there for self-improvement and to learn how to dance, not specifically to meet my beshert. I happily paid my money and went inside.

Dancing has never been my forte. I don't quite do the Elaine Dance from *Seinfeld*, but I'm no Jennifer Lopez either. That said, I've always loved to dance. So I came to do the wobble. I came to do the cha-cha slide. I came to do the cupid shuffle.

But as the teacher turned on the Michael Bublé soundtrack, I knew this wasn't going to be that kind of line dancing class. Instead, I learned to rhumba, mambo, and waltz. I learned to cha cha and swing. And did I have my work cut out for me! These dances aren't easy, and I was uncoordinated compared to most, if not all, of my fellow older participants.

The dance lessons were also infused with useful tips on how to prevent osteoporosis and preserve my hips, so I would be less likely to fall and break one. I rolled my eyes. But out of everyone there, guess who got a foot cramp? Yep, the youngest person in the room. A nice gentleman did offer to give me a foot rub in the lobby, which I politely declined.

During the break, I spent time talking to a handful of the thirty or so singles attending the class. Some had never been married. Some were divorced. Some were widows or widowers. Some had careers. Some had changed careers. Some had just started careers. Everyone had a story to tell about how he or she arrived, single, to class that day. I, too, shared my story.

After kibitzing for a little while longer, we went back inside to finish the class. For the remainder of the time, I laughed, I stumbled, and, contrary to my original intention, I became even more Elaine-like. I wasn't the only one either. When the woman behind me grumbled about how she wasn't doing the steps right, the elderly man next to her smiled and reassured her.

"It's OK," he said. "You're dancing to your own music."

And that was the lesson I was there to learn that day. In that old ballroom, in the lower level of a forlorn synagogue whose life seemed to have long since left it, I learned to dance to my own music, to live in the moment. I'm single. This is my new reality. And I need to start living my life and doing things I enjoy, not to meet someone, but just because.

As I said goodbye to the instructor and thanked her for teaching, a sixty-seven-year-old woman from the group gave me her business card and told me she runs a belly dancing class. I took the card and thought, "You know, that just might be my next stop."

So He Cheated . . . Does That Make Him a Bad Guy?

Cheater.

That is what I called him. The word effortlessly and thoughtlessly rolled off my tongue, the only label that came to mind as my husband admitted, unrepentantly, he was with and committed to another woman.

Undeniably, we had our problems. Major ones. A lack of mutual respect, divergent goals, little interest in each other's lives. An all-around distaste for one another. But I never thought he would be unfaithful. Not in a million years. Not this guy. Not someone I knew so well, for so long. Yet as I looked my adulterer husband in the eye, I was faced with reconciling a man's entire life with his recent behavior. Yes, in my estimation, he had done something reprehensible. But did that make him a categorically bad person?

It was recently posed to me that if character is defined by our actions, then my husband is, by default, a bad guy. Even as I write these words, I recoil at the thought, cringe at such an absolute notion of humanity. The statement represents a line in the sand, a black and white classification of good versus evil, and is a concept with which I am in conflict and wrestle to understand.

Hermann Hesse, in his novel *Siddhartha*, tells the allegorical tale of the Buddha as a young man struggling to comprehend such dichotomy. A member of the high Brahmin caste in India, Siddhartha feels so unsettled in his teachings that he renounces his scholarly life to wander in search of peace and enlightenment. His journey, which leads him to a life of asceticism, greed, and hedonism, then back to asceticism, illustrates that a man's life is the sum total of his experiences and that it is in the course of searching where true meaning lies.

During the twenty-six years I have known my ex-husband, I witnessed this man work his mind and body to the core to provide for his family's well-being. I watched him hold his children in his arms minutes after they were born and revel in their accomplishments as they reached milestone after milestone and achieved their own hard-earned goals. I saw the way he once looked at me, with only love in his eyes, and how he bared his soul when he was vulnerable.

Circumstances are different now. Yet history remains.

Every day our interactions impact others. With even so little as a glance, our essence is left behind, and we live on forever in someone else's memory. The longer we interact, the more memories we create and amass. Our lives become a collective memory, and how others perceive us is our undeniable legacy.

We all have moments in our lives that plague us. Moments we wish we could erase, those haunting whispers that torment us in our most quiet hour. Committing adultery is the worst kind of betrayal. It is cowardly, spineless, and a personal affront to the person we once cared for and protected. The day I learned my husband lied to me, scorned me, my innocence was corrupted forever. But I will not allow his actions to harden my heart, to rob me of the life we once lived together, in both good times and in bad.

Yesterday, I wished my ex-husband a happy birthday because I believe his forty-four years are worthy of acknowledgment. He has done things in his life of which he may now, or one day in time, not be proud. We both have. But he has also positively affected the lives of many, mine included.

For whatever reason, his journey has brought him to where he is today. He makes his arguments, though I may not agree or necessarily understand them. But it is not my place to do so. I am on my own path, in large part because of the time we shared. To arbitrarily define my ex-husband, to negate the cumulative impact of our lives on one another, would mean staying anchored to the follies of our pasts and denying my newfound freedom.

And that is not something I am willing to do.

When a Wife Becomes the Other Woman in Her Own Marriage

"When I'm with you, I feel like I'm cheating on her."

I winced as I retreated, needing a moment to reconcile my husband's derisive statement.

"I'm the other woman?" I pleaded. How could that be?

I was a faithful wife. Dutiful. A partner in the business of our lives, as my husband frequently described me to others with what I believed at the time high praise, especially to a woman who, though once career-minded, stayed home to raise her children. Yet somehow, someway, I had become the detestable, an intruder in a life I had only days earlier called my own.

At that moment, I recalled the 1992 film *Single White Female* in which a new roommate assumes the identity of the woman whose apartment she shares. I believed my ex-husband's mistress to be the same. She injected herself into my life and took my place. Stole my husband and my lifestyle, and today even creepily shares an apartment with him in the same complex where we once lived as a family.

Years later, I finally understand my husband's words. While a wife, I played many parts. But there was one part for which I apparently needed an understudy—his beloved. I loved my husband. But I was no longer in love with him, nor was he with me. Not for a long time. We both felt it.

There are many different types of love. But for a marriage to endure, to stand the test of time, to survive illness, financial troubles, and whatever other challenges life throws at us, that one indescribable feeling, the feeling we dismissively categorize in the catchall of love, needs to be present. And not only present, omnipresent, pervading every aspect of a couple's life together.

Love, as the saying goes, is in the air.

I knew that love once. Long ago. Now, as I date, a part of my consciousness separates from the sea of activity around me. I absorb. I assess. Could I love this person? Is there a hint of the indescribable in the air, right here, right now?

Most of the time, I already have my answer: no.

I believe the potential for love can be sensed within moments. If that potential is not there, I do not believe it ever can be. At least not in the way I would want. Yes, we can grow to love someone we like. We can respect them. Feel attraction. But experience passion? I remain skeptical.

I have been advised by some to settle for less. Accept the realities of my situation. You are divorced. You are a single mother of three. You are in your forties. You are, you are, you are . . .

I may be many things, but hopeless is not one of them.

My children are vacationing this week in San Francisco with their dad and the other-other woman. Yesterday, the kids called to tell me about their visit to Alcatraz, the notorious penitentiary known for its perfect record for unsuccessful escapes.

As I listened to them recount their day, I remembered my now ex-husband's refusal to take me there when I suggested it during a long weekend away. Somehow, when it came to me and my wants, there was never enough time, enthusiasm, or interest. My children, aware of my desire to also see the landmark, offered to return with me. My heart warmed at their thoughtfulness, and then I felt regret.

A healthy marriage should be filled with that same sentiment. For years, mine was not. I spent far too long accepting less than I wanted or deserved. In return, I gave less attention, less devotion, and less passion—to love and to life. I lived in solitude as a result, watching the world go on without me from the microcosm I created at home.

Prisons are frequently referred to as correctional institutions, psychiatric hospitals as mental institutions. And, of course, there is matrimony, which is oftentimes described as the institution of marriage. The Britannica Dictionary defines an institution as "a place where an organization takes care of people for a usually long period of time." The marriage I knew did no such thing.

Visiting Alcatraz remains on my bucket list. Except that the next time I visit San Francisco, it will be as a single woman. I still believe in marriage and hope to be married again one day, though to a man who can be a loving partner to me and I to him. I no longer live in the confining prison of a loveless marriage, truly one of the lucky ones able to escape.

And freedom has never felt so good.

Three Years After My Husband Left Me, I Finally Came Out of the Closet

It's always the same. Just when I think "it" is finally over, something leaps out in front of me as if to say, "Not so fast, sister."

I caught them out of the corner of my eye. Shoes. Not mine. His. I don't know how I missed them. Yet there they sat on the floor of my closet, as if they still belonged there but now strangely out of place.

In the end, it was me who was to blame for the oversight. Oh well. I'd done my best under the circumstances.

"Throw it all away," my husband had ordered shortly after announcing he was divorcing me. "I already have everything I want."

Telling words.

Dutifully, I did as he asked, perhaps in a last-ditch and surely misguided effort to appease him. Make him want me back, "good wife" that I was.

I took it all—suits, shirts, ties, tees, jeans, and shoes—filling bag after bag with his personal effects, donating them to charity days later. I imagined some less fortunate soul wearing the Hermès tie I bought him for his birthday, naively believing its previous owner had died. What other explanation could there be for discarding something so valuable?

When I was done, I surveyed my work. I don't know why, but I thought I'd feel a sense of relief when I was finished. I didn't. I only felt worse as I stared disbelievingly at the physical manifestation of that now inescapable void in my gut.

As I looked around my house at the carefully framed photographs gracing nearly every tabletop and bookshelf (of our engagement party, of our wedding day, of that day we spent strolling along the cobblestone streets of Portofino), at the artwork on the walls (the lithograph we overpaid for at an art gallery because its subject looked strikingly like our young nephew and the painting from a celebrated Aboriginal artist that my husband gave me one Valentine's Day), at the trinkets we collected during our many travels and time spent living abroad (Murano glass, Buddha statues, jade carvings), even at the martini glasses that now sat collecting dust in a cabinet—I realized my work had only just begun.

In anticipation of a dinner guest—a man I was seeing during those first months following my separation—I felt an urgency to take those memories to task. In the name of not making my date uncomfortable (though it was really me who would be), I went from room to room in the days before his arrival, painstakingly scouring every surface for evidence of my former married life, hiding all that I could in that newly empty closet, out of sight and mind.

What I failed to anticipate was that walls talk. They remember. They recall the way life used to be, filled with vibrant family dinners, harried breakfasts, lazy mornings, and family movie nights.

Theirs wasn't a conversation I was ready to hear, and I muffled those whispers the only way I knew how—by tuning them out. I began eating alone at mealtime, standing next to the kitchen sink or sitting at the kitchen island. I no longer slept in my bed and began sleeping everywhere except my bed—with my children, on the couch, or in the guest room. I stopped watching TV because we used to watch it together.

Somehow though, without my even realizing, my clothes gradually began to overtake the empty rungs in what was once our closet. My plate made its way to the dinner table. And I returned to my bedroom, first spending countless months sleeping on top of the bed instead of in it.

I'd like to say the night that I pulled back the covers and climbed in was a monumental one. It wasn't. It was, to put it simply, time.

During my divorce, I had negotiated that our three children and myself would remain in our marital home until they each graduated from high school. But before the ink was even dry on my decree, I began feeling as if I might've made a grievous mistake. That I'd inadvertently placed myself under a veritable house arrest, depriving myself of the fresh start I suddenly craved in a different house, one devoid of memories of life before divorce.

Alyosha the Baptist said it best in Aleksandr Solzhenitsyn's novel *One Day in the Life of Ivan Denisovich:* "You should rejoice that you're in prison. Here you have time to think about your soul."

And that I have.

I never did finish packing away the rest of those knick-knacks I had at first sought to hide. Instead, I picked and chose. Out with some of the old, in with some of the new.

As it turned out, everything did have its place, myself included. It was only a matter of finding it.

With that, I picked up those old, abandoned shoes, dropped them in a bag for donation, and came out of that closet for good.

Do You Really Care? Now Ask Yourself Why You Do

"Why do you care?"

I recently posed this question to a friend of mine. She had just gotten through telling me that after a string of great dates with a guy, he began to fade. Though they continued to communicate, he stopped asking her out, his once frequent texts began to wane, and he was active on the same popular dating site where they first met. She liked this guy—a lot—and was rather upset, judging by her demeanor.

But her words spoke otherwise as she claimed she was over him and moving on. I knew better.

"Great," I said. "So you're online then?"

She gave me a funny look.

"Well, not exactly," she conceded. "My profile is up, but I hardly ever log in because I want him to think that I'm busy. Or that I met someone else."

I was confused. Because any time a relationship of mine came to a close, I put myself back online sooner rather than later, believing the best remedy for a hole in the heart was to find someone who would fit better to fill it.

"So you're not really putting yourself back out there, only pretending you are?" I asked, making sure I understood her logic.

"Yes," she confirmed with a sheepish half-smile.

"But he's looking," I reminded her. "And besides, you just said you were fine, which, obviously, you're not, and you do still care what he thinks."

What I wasn't sure of was whether she had acknowledged to herself why.

In situations like this, most of us don't admit to ourselves we still have strong feelings for someone even though we speak and behave to the contrary.

It's an art—looking like we don't care when we actually do.

My ex-husband is the master of indifference. I like to think of him as Dr. Jekyll and Mr. Hyde. Whenever he speaks to me without an audience, he's pleasant. Even, dare I say, nice. But if his significant other is anywhere in the vicinity, he goes out of his way to be nasty. Or he's cold, proving to her his disdain for me and my insignificance in his life. Then when we're alone, he's back again to Mr. Nice Guy.

He cares.

When I first learned my husband was leaving me, and for another woman no less, I cared. A lot. To the point where I made it my mission to find out every last painful detail about the woman who stole my husband from me, when their relationship started, and what they were doing as a couple.

I admit I employed some pretty sneaky tactics and high-level snooping techniques to garner the information I wanted. Why?

I cared.

At the time, it seemed pretty obvious to me that my husband did not. Phone calls to his girlfriend from our family room with me nearby, his purchase of gifts for her that he didn't go out of his way to hide and, for the grand finale, arranging to meet her in Paris before returning with her to the country he was now declaring his permanent home. He was brazen. He wanted me to know. He wanted to punish me.

He cared.

I remember standing in the driveway during those last few moments of the week my husband came home for his father's funeral, just a little over a month after I found the lingerie. I was still whirling from the events that had transpired over the previous days, days that I thought I could use to win him back by helping him plan the funeral and by being a supportive wife. What is that saying about doing good deeds?

I had always wanted to go to Paris, and we spoke many times about going there together. Then I overheard him talking to his girlfriend after the burial; he had a business trip to Paris scheduled for a few days later and was planning to fly her there from Hong Kong to be with him. It was supposed to be me who was on that plane.

During our marriage, I never hung up the phone without telling my husband I loved him, probably the lasting effect of losing a parent so suddenly when I was an adolescent. The same applied when he left on business trips, with me always saying I loved him before he walked out the door. But over that fateful week, my husband told me for the past however many months that he felt as though he had been saying something he no longer meant.

As I watched my husband walk down our driveway for the last time before officially separating, I wished him a safe trip as I always did. I was in shock, as well as emotionally distraught, a feeling that unbeknownst to me then, would last for many months to come. For the very last time, I told my husband I loved him. I had said it countless times over the preceding days, my heart breaking further with each silent rebuke.

I'll never forget it, though. Before getting into the car to go to the airport, my husband stopped and turned toward me. Then he said what we had both been taking for granted for so long: "I love you too."

My ex-husband has not said those words to me since, nor I to him. Among the men I dated during the early years following our separation, I spoke those four words to only one person, under pressure, and not because I meant them. I didn't. When I left that relationship for the last time, I felt relief, underscoring further that I never felt the same for him as he did for me.

I rarely think of that man. If I do, it's not in a way that brings back any fondness for me or interest in seeing where he is in his life.

I don't care.

I no longer care about my husband's new life either. Only to the extent that it affects my children. When my children try to offer me details about their father, I'm legitimately ambivalent. In fact, I tell them it's not my concern.

I don't care.

I venture to say that my husband was right when all along he said that I was the one who pushed him away. I did. I had fallen out of love with him years earlier, and it showed. In retrospect, how much I cared when my husband left me had more to do with ego than with love.

Love is painful. It makes us hurt. Feel exposed. Vulnerable. It's a risk, one with high stakes but a huge payout. If you don't like those odds, it's easier to act as though you don't care. To take measures to show you don't care. Believe you don't care. That way, you can't get hurt.

But, if despite all you do, you still find yourself caring—thinking about someone a lot, keeping tabs on them, posturing, seeking out others who remind you of that person, or recreating a familiar set of circumstances with another—ask yourself why.

You may be surprised at your answer.

We Welcome with Love . . . Our New Step-Monster

Ben Harrison: "Mommy . . ."
Jackie Harrison: "What, sweetie?"
Ben Harrison: "If you want me to hate her I will."
—*Stepmom*, 1998

It is with great . . . sorrow, anger, indifference, or some combination of the three, I'm not quite sure, that I announce our upcoming family addition. No, it's not a baby. Yet. It's my children's stepmom.

Very recently, though I can't say exactly when because I'm not privy to such information, my ex-husband became engaged to the woman he's been seeing, the woman he left me for. I heard the news from my kids. They found out as their dad passed around his iPhone at a family dinner a couple of months back, sporting a picture of his fiancée's engagement ring for all to admire.

But I really can't complain because it's not like they didn't already have a heads up about the situation. Their future stepmom took care of that during a previous visit when, without their father present, she giddily (and provokingly?) said to my older daughter, "I think your dad is going to ask me to marry him. What do you think I should say?" Minutes later, I was hit with a barrage of frantic texts from the backseat of their dad's car as they attempted to mask their hysterics from him.

Until now, my ex-husband's significant other has held the dubious honor of being the other woman, a title that accurately denotes her well-deserved status as a homewrecker, the most unwanted of intruders. A title that categorically trumps the positions of invasive in-law and overbearing family member. Now, as she usurps the ubiquitous title of stepmom, devastating my children, I know there's not a damn thing I can do about it. Or is there?

It's no secret to my ex-husband, his future bride, and, frankly, to anyone else who will listen that my children and I aren't her biggest fans. She does things to tick the kids off, intentionally or unintentionally (I can't always be sure), and they aren't very forgiving. Neither am I, for that matter. But she keeps going about her day, living her life, and even appears happier for it as my children become more irritated and upset. The old saying about how hating a person is like drinking rat poison and expecting someone else to die is true. So really, who are the victims in this scenario?

Today, I stand at a crossroads. Either I can sit back and allow my children to continue disparaging this woman, or I can facilitate her inevitable transition into their lives. These children can't help but blame their dad's fiancée for destroying their parents' marriage. In reality, though, she was only a symptom, even a catalyst, but certainly not the cause. When a marriage is strong, nothing can shake it from its foundation. Ours was anything but that.

I didn't get to choose the woman who will become my children's stepmom. But I can choose how I regard her publicly and ultimately affect how my children view her. I can't promise that I will ever be her friend. I'm not that progressive, but really, nobody knows what the future holds. My task is difficult; I must swallow my pride and pay a modicum of respect to a woman I disrespect and dislike. But for better or for worse, till death (or divorce) do my ex-husband and her part, she will be in my children's lives.

Everybody has good qualities, even her. And, though I hate to admit it, she's not a monster. By acknowledging my children's stepmom, by paying her that respect, it's not she who I hold in high regard, but my children. So for them, I will do what I once believed unthinkable: I will accept her.

If Mama Was Married

I think my kids are trying to get rid of me. Really. I feel like the stage mother Rose in the 1962 film version of the Broadway musical *Gypsy*. They say it's taking me way too long to find a husband. Ha! Clearly, they haven't spent time dating online. And how long is too long, I wonder?

I'm frequently reminded their dad is already engaged and told I should be too. It's just that easy, they argue. I'm a good sport, though, and I never bring up the unfair advantage he had finding his betrothed, the head start he unanimously claimed while we were still married. But that's another story. And I certainly don't want to burst their bubble that I'm their mother, not their daughter, so they can't actually give me away.

I'm pretty sure nagging your mom to find a new spouse isn't typical for children of single parents. I, for one, chased away more than a few of my mother's suitors when I was a young teen. After all, who wanted some graying middle-aged guy hanging around? Oh, how things have changed . . . But, in all honesty, sometimes I think my children aren't looking for a husband for me but, rather, a stepfather for them. I only wonder if they understand what that means exactly.

These requests usually come on the heels of a visit with their dad. There's always a whirlwind of excitement during the days leading up to a trip and an action-packed, fun-filled love fest when they're together. But there's no afterglow. No basking in the glory of divorce-directed visitation. Only a disappointing return to the house where their dad once lived and the familial void they now perceive in his absence.

After my father died, I felt a similar vacancy. Although my perception, left in the wake of a parent's death, not a divorce, definitely seems more profound in comparison due to its permanency. Even so, I do have a definite sense of what they feel. And I don't ever suggest because their father is alive that hope exists he will return to our home one day. That's never going to happen. But, unlike my brother and me, they do get to see their father, and he remains very much a part of their lives.

Yet I still get the sense they think, particularly my nine-year-old son, that there's someone out there who will be able to assume their father's role quickly and easily. Nope, not happening. I know that from my own experience as a stepchild—and mine was a good one, most of the time. What they want is a magic potion, a quick fix to relieve them of their pain. That's not going to happen either.

After my father died, I remember looking forward to moving to a new house and having a fresh start. Then one day, I overheard my paternal grandmother tell my mother about how I was mistaken in my belief that a new setting would instantaneously make me feel better. She was right. That peacefulness came slowly, minute-by-minute, hour-by-hour, and day-by-day over the course of a lifetime.

So I tell my children I'm not looking for a new father for them. They already have one, and he loves them very much. Instead, I tell them I'm looking for a life partner for me, and not necessarily a husband at that. I would like to get remarried one day. But it will be a choice that I make based on the conglomeration of numerous factors. What I'm looking for is best defined as a friend with benefits. Not for me, for them. This person will be their friend first and foremost and, hopefully, bring to the equation those benefits lacking in their relationships with their own father, whether the result of long-distance parenting or otherwise.

These children are going to be grown before I blink an eye. They will go off to college, graduate school if they choose, pursue their careers, and, with luck, find that one unique person to love, who loves them, and with whom they want to share their lives. They will hopefully live their lives as honest, hard-working, decent people with the values I try each day to instill in them. When these things happen, I will know I have done my part raising them well. Yes, I will always be their mom. I will always love them and be available to support them whenever they need me and to share in their joys as they meet them throughout their lives.

But when they leave my home, I don't want to look around at my life gone by, reminiscing each day and longing for what once was. I don't want to live in the shadows of my past. I want to turn to the person next to me and look forward to the bright, beautiful day that awaits us. Together, we will move into the future, as Ronald Reagan once said, "to begin the journey that will lead me into the sunset of my life."

And as we know, sunsets can be the most beautiful time of day.

Hush, Little Cheater, I Won't Say a Word . . .

"I want to thank you," I said to my husband's personal assistant on that ordinary afternoon when I called him at work, as I had done countless times before.

"Oh?" she asked. "What for?"

"For making all of those dinner reservations, for booking all of those plane tickets, and for reserving all of those hotel rooms for my husband . . . and his mistress," I said.

The phone went silent, followed by a nervous laugh on the other end.

"I'm sorry," she said. Then quietly, "I'm very sorry."

How many times had I called my husband, now my ex, at his office? His assistant knew he had a wife and three children. A home. A life. And yet she always remained so composed, so poised, as she politely transferred my calls, passed along my messages, all while conveniently looking the other way. One could argue that she was a subordinate, expected to follow her boss's instructions. But how about an anonymous note? Something, anything, to alert me to the fact my husband was being unfaithful to me, disrespecting me, and, most importantly, potentially putting my health, and my life, at risk.

Was she obligated to tell me? We are, after all, both women. Don't we belong to some unspoken sisterhood, some secret society of sorts? Did her knowledge somehow make her culpable for the despair my children and I would eventually suffer? Or, even worse, the potential health risks to which I was being exposed, as I believed my husband was committed only to me? I, fortunately, was unscathed in that regard. I am truly one of the lucky ones.

Years earlier, my husband and I had dinner with one of his friends and his wife. I had never met them before, but they seemed like such a loving couple. I envied the way he looked at her, the way he held her hand at the table, the way he asked her throughout the evening if she was OK, if she was enjoying herself. They had young children, but it was obvious they were still in love.

His concern for her well-being, as it turned out, was justified. She had recently undergone major surgery, a full hysterectomy, while still in her late thirties. It was a terrible thing, she explained to me in the ladies' room, how she had contracted an infection while swimming. Nothing would cure the disease that ravaged her reproductive system. Surgery, she explained, was her only option.

I would later hear a rumor that, no, swimming was not the culprit at all but rather her husband. As a result of his philandering, he had given her an STI, sadly necessitating the premature loss of her fertility.

It is amazing how looks can be so deceiving. What I at first perceived as a loving relationship was, I imagine, a case of intense guilt, presumably as he tried to salvage what was left of his broken marriage. From what I understand, they are still together. Her reasons, altogether unknown to me, are also none of my business.

Still, I cannot help but wonder, what if someone had known of this man's extramarital activities, perhaps his personal assistant, a friend, or their nanny? Would any of these people have been affirmatively charged with the responsibility for telling his unknowing spouse of her husband's indiscretions? It is easy to point a finger and emphatically say yes. But actually coming forward and taking the risk of telling the one suffering the betrayal is a weighty responsibility, especially if you have never met the aggrieved spouse before and likewise are unaware whether the husband and wife are complicit in some sort of "other arrangement." As we know, open marriages do exist and are not uncommon. However, in this case, it seemed highly unlikely.

I dated a married man once. As soon as I discovered his "secret," I bowed out of the relationship, which was in its embryonic stage. But it raised the question for me: what was my obligation? Must I now become the Norma Rae for infidelity because I was unlucky enough to meet a man who presumably lied to both his wife and me?

Telling a spouse her husband is cheating may arguably be the "right" thing to do. I personally would have wanted someone to tell me. To this day, I still don't know when my husband's affair began and likely never will. I only recently learned he knew his mistress a lot longer than I once thought. Now I question whether there were others before her, how many, and for how long.

In the situation of my husband's friend and his wife, the wife chose to stay married. But maybe had someone told her that her husband was cheating, her health would not have been compromised as it was.

Still, injecting oneself into someone else's marriage is a delicate task and a precarious place to be. Maybe that makes me a coward for not telling the wife of the man I was dating that he and I had been involved. But things have a way of snowballing. Although I would not be the sole person responsible for ending their marriage (if it did end), I could be a catalyst. Contributing to the breakup of a family, even if only as a messenger, is a lot to live with.

When I first discovered my husband was cheating, I called his mistress and confronted her. She neither confessed nor denied their involvement, merely telling me that she knew him, that they were friends. "Good friends." When I did finally elicit a confession from my husband (never an apology, not to this day), I called her again, requesting that she take a step back and let us attempt to repair our twenty-four-year relationship. She summarily refused. I sent her a Facebook message as well, which she ignored. Perhaps, had she left the place where she didn't belong—my husband's bed—our marriage might have been saved. But she saw to it that we would never find out.

When I learned the man I was seeing was married, I removed myself. If they truly were unhappy, if their marriage was genuinely riddled with problems, as he purported, then one of them would eventually leave. That, I believe, is a decision to be made between a husband and wife.

Having been both the jilted wife and the other woman, albeit unwittingly, I can say with certainty neither is an admirable title to hold. Both positions left me damaged. But as the other woman, I often question whether I did enough to absolve myself of responsibility, even though I was an unsuspecting actor. Was I proactive enough once I knew the depth of my involvement? Did I need to be proactive at all?

It was recently posed to me that husbands who cheat put their wives in peril, exposing them to potentially fatal diseases, such as HIV and HPV, the leading cause of cervical cancer. This is a legitimate argument for informing, no doubt. We are not merely talking about emotions anymore, even though these, too, can be psychologically devastating. In this regard, we as women have a communal responsibility to look out for those of us who may be in the process of being unknowingly victimized.

I have received a fair amount of criticism regarding my decision not to tell this woman about my brief relationship with her husband. But I still maintain that the degree to which we interfere in someone else's marriage is a very personal choice and one that weighs on me daily.

As of today, I have not come forward. I cannot say what tomorrow will bring. No choice is right or wrong; it rests in what we, as women, can bear. And, I am here to say, the cross is a heavy one.

Cheater: One of the 'Goodfellas,' Only Misunderstood

"Are you fucking my husband?"

It was the question I asked when I called her for the first time (yes, there would be other times), her being the woman who was fucking my husband.

I didn't actually need her to tell me, though. The vacant look on my husband's face alone during the week following his announcement that he was "done with our marriage" was really the only proof I ever needed.

When my husband learned that I had called his good friend (how she described her relationship with my husband to me), I was chastised for embarrassing him. He compared my apparent classlessness to that of Henry Hill's wife Karen in the 1990 film *Goodfellas* as she rang random buzzers in the lobby of her husband's mistress's apartment building yelling, "I'm going to tell everybody that walks in this building that in 2R, Rossi, you're nothing but a whore."

Over the coming weeks, my husband's good friend and I had several more conversations (most, but not all, precipitated by me). In one, I attempted to reason with her to leave my husband alone. In another, I mockingly questioned whether she preferred to be called a whore or a piece of ass. She chose piece of ass before hanging up on me.

My attempts fell on deaf ears as she told me, in no uncertain terms, that no matter what I did to try and save my marriage, it would not affect her relationship with my husband.

As time would tell, she would be right.

More than my husband's actions, what I found most curious was his mistress's lack of remorse, remorse for her part in a marriage's end, especially where three young children were involved.

Why did she not care? Why did she choose to believe my husband when he told her he and I were separated for two years when we weren't?

I was quick to point a finger. Call her a homewrecker. A whore. But was the fault only hers? Or even hers at all?

With those questions in mind, I summoned the courage on one sunny afternoon to type the text I had been waiting for so long to write.

"Situation still the same?" I casually asked of the married man I unwittingly dated a year earlier.

At first, he didn't recognize my number, having deleted my contact information.

"I'm saved," I thought, "from myself." I was already regretting what I had done. Better I let a sleeping dog lie.

But as the day progressed, curiosity got the best of him, and he called. When I saw the number come up, I panicked and sent the call straight to voicemail.

Recognizing my name and voice from the outgoing message, he texted again.

No, his situation was not the same. He was available.

We spoke on the phone, and over the next few weeks, we exchanged sporadic texts until finally setting a time to see one another.

I chose to believe. Look the other way. Take what he said at face value.

Over drinks and then dinner, we reacquainted ourselves with one another, sharing stories about work and family. Tales of a wife mostly focused on her children from a previous marriage, her vanity, and interests that did not appear to interest him.

I asked what specifically about his situation had changed from when we first met.

Physical separation. Financial planning. A desire to move on.

And what about his situation hadn't changed? That he was likely lying to me, yet again.

Only this go-around, I knew better.

"You know, what you did wasn't very nice," I said, speaking of how he had lied to me about his marital status.

"It's not like I did it for the sake of it," he explained.

This statement I believed.

Within every lie, there exists its opposite—the truth. In my eyes, this was it. The truth I saw that evening came in the form of a man desperately looking for the attention and appreciation he was obviously not feeling at home, likely why he exuded such warmth when we first met and the chemistry between us was so heated.

Not surprising. If we aren't careful, marriage can become the loneliest place on Earth. I know.

Single life can often feel the same way. I know that as well. It was likely that loneliness which served as the impetus for my not so innocent-innocent inquiry as to this man's marital status and, I assume, what also inspired my husband's mistress to aggressively pursue a man living and working thousands of miles from his family, similarly starved for affection as a consequence.

Today I question whether my husband's mistress is the same homewrecker I once thought. My husband and I seemed to do a pretty good job wrecking the home we built together without any of her help.

As for me, did I feel guilty about spending an evening with a man I suspected still to be married?

Surprisingly, no.

For one night that didn't lead to another (it's hard to build anything on lies), I saw my ex-husband in another man, myself in my husband's mistress, and in his mistress an understanding of why some women gravitate to men who are already spoken for.

It's easy to say with conviction that cheating should never happen. Accepting why it often does is what remains a challenge.

Beyond Divorce: When Salt No Longer Hurts a Wound

"Scar tissue is stronger than regular tissue. Realize the strength, move on." —Henry Rollins

As someone who has written about divorce and single parenting for the past eighteen months—about the process, the highs, the lows, about the self-discovery that comes from transitioning into a new phase of life in middle age—I have been struggling in recent weeks to collect my thoughts into yet another coherent essay that best describes my present state of mind a little more than three years after my husband announced he was leaving me.

I have made many attempts, crafted countless essays, only to leave them unfinished, collecting dust, if you will, as computer files I will revisit one day in the future, or perhaps never again. An article detailing a humorous dating story, a retelling of a spat with my ex-husband over our different parenting styles, a rehashing of the pain I endured as he extricated himself from our life together. Yet, for whatever reason, I have been experiencing difficulty assigning personal significance to these familiar anecdotes as I once did.

Up until now, my writing has been synonymous with my healing or, more accurately, the storm that has been raging inside me. Long periods of turbulence surrounded by shorter periods of calm, each of which grew inversely proportional to the other as time went on until, finally, that period of turbulence became nothing more than a distant memory even though timewise that distance has not been so vast.

It is an odd sensation knowing that I am now strong enough to leave the pain of my marriage's end behind. All of the heartache, the hurt, and the confusion, as I spent years struggling to solidify my new role and identity as a divorced single mother and, more importantly, as the strong, independent woman I did not always believe I could be. All of it is now under control. Today, I am able to wrap it up, put it in a safe place, and move along on my path without always carrying such a heavy burden with me.

That is not to say I will ever be clear of the scars my divorce has left behind. Rather, only free of its shackles. I embrace the fact that I am forever changed—and for the better. There have been no mistakes along the way, only lessons to be learned and self-realization to be embraced.

The turning point came last week when a close friend admitted to withholding information she knew about my ex-husband. Nearly a year ago, she learned he attempted to do something that, had it come to pass, would have been, at the very least, uncomfortable for my children and me, though I am fairly certain that was not his immediate intention and, more likely, a consequence of my ex-husband trying to satisfy his own needs.

Not sure at the time if she should tell me about what she had discovered or keep it to herself, my friend asked both her mother (who knows me) and a mutual friend of ours for their advice. My friend's mother opined that my knowing would serve no end (at least, not a good one), while our mutual friend argued I should be told.

I was not.

As I listened to my friend relay this information nearly ten months after she learned it, I could feel my blood pressure beginning to rise. My immediate inclination was to be angry. Not only at my ex-husband but also at my friend for taking it upon herself to determine what was best for me. The problem was I really was not all that annoyed. Yet I played the part—well, I would like to think—because, at first, I believed that is what my response should have been.

I remained calm as my friend justified her decision, listening to her explain, and rightfully so, that what my ex was attempting to do was not something I could control. Nor was it something I could have prevented. Knowing about it could have only served to further weaken an already fragile relationship, one that we needed to strengthen for the benefit of our children. She thought there was no advantage to rubbing salt in an already deep wound.

In the midst of my divorce, as well as in its immediate aftermath, I would have likely gotten into an argument with my friend over how I believed she betrayed me, as well as with our other mutual friend for keeping this secret, even though it was not hers to reveal. Next, I would have, in a fit of anger, picked up the phone and called my ex-husband out on his behavior at once.

Not this time.

Instead, I politely ended the conversation and kept what I had learned to myself. Yes, I did speak with my ex-husband later that evening, but not about what I was told. In fact, I am not certain if I will ever bring up the topic because, first, it never came to fruition and, second, doing so will only incite hostility. But it is perhaps my third and final reason for remaining silent that makes my decision most compelling—I am actually not bothered by what he did.

Which got me thinking: have I finally moved beyond my divorce?

My divorce left me injured. But slowly, ever so slowly, I healed. Though I will forever bear my scars, I am humbled my wound was not a mortal one. And that is the inherent beauty of the human condition. Personal closure can only come when we acknowledge and accept such truth. After three years, I have.

Are Single Parents All Created Equal?

I recently wrote an article titled "10 Things This Single Mom Wants Her Kids to Know," in which I discussed raising my three children post-divorce almost entirely on my own.

My now ex-husband has been living overseas for years, beginning (almost to the day) two years prior to when we officially separated during January of 2012. Although we legally agreed to joint custody, the reality is, due to my ex's proximity (or lack thereof) to our children, I retain full physical custody of them most of the time. So when I titled my article and referred to myself as a single mom (which I, with every fiber of my being, believe I am), I didn't anticipate being met with criticism from others who argue I am not, in fact, a single mother because my children's father continues to play a role in their lives.

To that, I say bullshit.

My ex-husband and I are, for the most part, amicable, though we still occasionally hit bumps in the road like so many other divorced couples who parent children from two separate homes, ours being located some 8,000 miles apart.

My ex-husband communicates with our children almost daily via FaceTime, text, or email. He either visits or travels with them during most major school holidays and for floating days every couple of months or so. He pays support—to them and me.

I, in turn, stay flexible, accommodating last-minute trips so he can see the kids whenever he is able.

We both love our children.

Our situation "works." Is it a perfect one? No. Are there worse situations? Yes. Are there better ones? Yes to that as well. Am I a single mom? Well, I guess that all depends on how the term "single mom" is defined.

If you ask me, I will tell you I am a single mom—with an emphatic yes.

I have debated this topic on numerous occasions with my own mom, once a single mom herself. She has since remarried and has been married for more than twenty-five years, but from the time I was thirteen years old and my brother ten when my father suffered a massive heart attack and died, she raised us alone. And by alone, I mean without financial assistance, little money, and limited emotional support from family and friends. After being a homemaker for the entire duration of her marriage, following my father's death, my mom returned to work as an administrative assistant in order to make ends meet.

My mom's single parenting experience and mine are by no means the same. I acknowledge and appreciate that. I lived through both (though one as a child of a single mom), and I contend neither scenario is more representative of single parenthood than the other.

By way of comparison, my mother was a widow, and I am divorced. And my ex is still involved in his children's lives, whereas my father could no longer be. But, in many ways, our situations are not all that different. And it's these similarities, I argue, that make a divorced mom (or dad) also a single mom (or dad).

Leaving money out of the equation for just a moment, let me say that single parenting is a state of mind, regardless of how involved an ex-spouse is in his or her children's lives. And it's this state of mind that pervades every thought we as divorced parents have throughout each day. Divorced single parents are never at rest. Even when not physically with our children, we are mentally there, worried about them, particularly as we relinquish control and knowledge of our children's whereabouts to an ex-spouse.

Of course, there is a broad spectrum as to the level of comfort we feel when our children receive care from their other parent. Every family varies. But I venture to say, even in those best-case scenarios, regardless of how loving and capable the other parent is and the faith we have in them, a small part of us still feels trepidation when our children walk out the door. Not to mention that post-divorce feeling of no longer being included in what was once "family" time.

It defies logic then that the most difficult divorced single parenting moments often come when we are with our children. Those times when they long for their other parent, the one they no longer see as often or at all (or, in some cases, never saw to begin with), whether en route to the bathroom or at the kitchen table while eating breakfast before school or dinner after a long day. That parent who is late to or cannot attend every Little League game, piano recital, or school concert, or who never attends at all. How many of us would rather suffer such disappointment ourselves than watch our children endure it?

For a divorced single parent, time is not money.

It's also important to acknowledge the physical toll parenting after divorce takes. I would think, due to its obviousness, that it shouldn't require further explanation. Yet I often find it does, especially to those married parents who don't quite "get" the difference. From last-minute trips to doctors, dentists, and the ER, to late-night trips to the twenty-four-hour pharmacy and nursing sick kids home from school, from car trouble to carpooling with car trouble, to juggling play dates, school activities, and endless household chores, divorced single parents, when we are enjoying our parenting time, are parenting solo, meaning there is no partner there to . . . partner.

Add work, financial pressure, special needs (whether a parent's or a child's), and whatever else we can or cannot foresee, it should be easy to see how exhausting, both mentally and physically, a divorced single parent's life can be.

Not always.

Of course, if we are single parents by divorce, it's possible we weren't getting this support during our marriage, and that's why we are, among other reasons, no longer married. But it doesn't change the basic premise that we as divorced single parents may still not be getting what we need, what every human being needs at one time or another—an extra pair of hands, a hug, the security of having someone in our corner, or maybe, just maybe, a special someone who will hold us in their arms as we drift off to sleep.

Single parenting is a way of life, whether we are parenting our kids on our own full-time, part-time, or sometimes, during those times when our children are with their other parent, and we are "off" for the day, night, or week. Where our children sleep is merely a matter of geography.

No, not all single parents are created equal. Some of us have it easier than others and in different ways. Some of us have it more difficult and in different ways. We can debate until we are blue in the face what constitutes those "better" or "worse" situations. But what I bet most of us can agree on is, although we would never have wished the difficulties single parenting involves upon ourselves, we also wouldn't trade our lives for anyone else's.

Loving the One I Was With: My Last-Minute Romantic Getaway

Silence can be deafening.

I confess I often feel alone. But it's not often that I'm actually alone. This past weekend, I found myself alone in both mind and body. And I didn't like it. Not one bit.

It's spring break, and my children are on a five-night trip with my ex-husband. I'm happy for the kids. It's important they see their father, especially since he lives so far away. I don't begrudge them having their time together and was, dare I say it aloud, looking forward to the quiet.

But in the flurry of activity last week, I neglected to make travel arrangements for myself for the few days I would be on my own. The truth is I didn't make my own plans a priority because I believed I would welcome the break from the chaos.

How wrong I was.

When I went to sleep Thursday night after everyone had gone, I was suddenly faced with an uncomfortable quiet. Naturally, I've been home alone before. I've actually spent entire summers in my house by myself while the children were at sleepaway camp. But on that night, the quiet beat down my door anyway like an angry intruder, reminding me of the downside of divorce—loneliness. Aware that four more full days of isolation lay ahead while waiting for my children to return, I was becoming increasingly despondent.

When morning came, I resigned myself to using the time productively to catch up on errands, household chores, and neglected projects. As the morning wore on and I completed what I needed to do outside the house first, I returned home at lunchtime to attack the rest of my to-do list.

Alone in my kitchen eating a sandwich, the sun beamed through the window, telling of the beautiful weekend to come. Since nothing was pressing enough to keep me at home, and I was starting to feel as if I didn't want to be there, I stood up, hurried to my computer, and began searching for places to go. After perusing the airlines for last-minute deals and not finding any destinations that appealed to me, I switched to looking for the perfect spot within a three-hour radius by car.

Suddenly, the photo of a picturesque bed and breakfast in Cape May, New Jersey, popped up and practically called my name through the computer screen. With only one room left, I booked my stay right then and within less than an hour was on the road to a romantic weekend getaway, even if it would be by myself.

When I arrived, I knew I had chosen right. A historic city by the ocean, Cape May offered me solitude in an old, refurbished mansion within walking distance to quaint shops and restaurants and, of course, the beach. In my room on the third floor, appointed with antique furniture and a plush king bed, I began my stay with the satisfaction that I now have enough confidence and wherewithal to take affirmative steps toward caring for and comforting myself. If I'm going to be alone, I thought, I might as well do it on my terms.

When I went to dinner that first night in a lovely restaurant just down the street, both the maître d' and waiter expressed surprise I was eating by myself. This is a frequent reaction, I'm discovering, as I venture out more and more on my own. It's also a troubling one. Is a person traveling or dining alone really a pariah, necessitating the stares of disbelieving onlookers?

In my experience, unfortunately so.

I'm sad to say I, too, have been guilty of making those same snap judgments. When I was living within the security of my married life not all that long ago, I couldn't comprehend how my single brother would sometimes vacation by himself. But, as he explained to me again and again in what would become another unsuccessful attempt to diffuse my condescension, if he waited around for everyone else's schedule to coordinate with his own, he would never do the things he wanted to do.

I admit that I do prefer to be in the presence of others. Though I'm at times alone, I'm by no means a loner. But the reality is sometimes, by circumstance, I'm forced to be by myself. Most of my friends are either married or in long-term relationships. Even my single friends are constrained by their own hectic schedules and obligations. If I wait around for others, I will, without a doubt, lead a sedentary, unadventurous life.

I've already spent way too many days of my life waiting. My ex-husband left for college two years before I did, and I waited for him to visit on weekends and holidays. When we were married, he worked long hours while I eventually stayed home to raise our children, and I waited for him to come home each night. Years later, his career led him to Hong Kong a second time, and I waited for him to move back because I couldn't bear to move there again. One day, he decided he no longer wanted to be married, and there I was again, waiting, this time for him to change his mind. He never did.

My wait is finally over.

I would love nothing more than to always have at my disposal the company of my loved ones, good friends, or the man with whom I will one day share my life. Such a life is not yet my own. And it may never be. So here I am, confronting my loneliness head-on as it tries to betray my confidence and rob me of my independence. In my fight, I refuse to let silence be my victor, holding me captive with paralyzing fear and preventing me from doing all of the things I once enjoyed and still wish to.

To some, it may appear I was fleeing my surroundings, and perhaps there's some truth to that. My house is undeniably haunted, inhabited with the ghosts of a life gone by. On some days, it reeks of decay as I recount my contribution to the demise of the family life that I worked so hard to create. On those days, I simply cannot bear to be in the confines of my home's rotten stench a moment longer. But I'm usually unable to escape and remain chained to my past even as I struggle to urge myself into the land of the living.

It was only as I packed my bag in the still of my house Friday afternoon that I heard the whisper. But it wasn't from a ghost. The voice came from within, and it told me to forgive and love myself.

There's no silence if we choose to listen. Opportunity surrounds us all. If we listen closely, our inner voice will guide us through our most difficult days. Music will fill the air, even when there's no music playing.

So I listened intently. And I heard the music. Then, with the car radio turned up, I followed my heart and loved the one I was with—me.

Divorce Bread

Do you ever wonder what to do with those end pieces of bread nobody wants to eat?

Yesterday afternoon, I cleaned out my freezer. It was a project long overdue, and as I made my children lunch after they returned home from spring break with their dad, I decided I could no longer look at all those unfinished loaves of bread shoved haphazardly and misshapen among the chicken fingers and frozen vegetables for even a minute longer. With determined frenzy, I pulled out each of those tied up crumpled plastic bags of bread and began opening them one by one, separating those useless ends no one wants from any middle slices left behind by mistake.

As I headed for the garbage with the first two ends, I stopped mid-toss before throwing them away. I couldn't do it. The pieces were still perfectly edible, and I hate to waste good food. I knew they had to have another use. So instead of disposing of them, I went through all the abandoned loaves and put each of the ends back in one of the bags. After sorting, I was left with a complete loaf of bread made up only of ends. Placing the new loaf back in the freezer, I felt satisfied with my second-hand creation, even though I had no idea what I would do with it.

All day long, I thought about that loaf of bread. I was sure it had another life in its new form. I just had to figure out what it was. I thought maybe the children and I could go to the park and feed the ducks. Of course, at thirteen, twelve, and nine, I wasn't altogether certain how eager they would still be to do that. I considered turning the crust side inward and using the slices for sandwiches, hoping the kids wouldn't notice or complain. In truth, though, I knew they would notice, and listening to them protest wouldn't be worth the effort. I even considered using the ends to soak up grease at the bottom of a meatloaf pan. But meatloaf isn't really a dinner my children or I enjoy. All in all, none of these solutions seemed quite right.

I spent the remainder of the afternoon opening suitcases and sorting through dirty laundry. The children were supposed to go back out with their dad late afternoon to see a Mets game, sitting in his law firm's seats close behind the dugout. The next day, he would return home to Hong Kong and wasn't scheduled to see the children for another three weeks.

The kids had fun on their trip as always, but I could already feel the tension rising that afternoon as they anticipated their dad's impending departure. As I tried to get my kids back on track for school the next day during those few short hours at home, directing them to study and complete unfinished homework, my older daughter responded to my perceived nagging by telling me how she doesn't like to come home after a vacation with her father. Understandable. Home is reality.

Standing before her, I represented all of the responsibilities she has to shoulder, and, in her defense, there are a lot. Between a rigorous academic schedule, extracurricular activities, and sports, her days are exhausting. I reminded her life isn't a vacation. Otherwise, there would be no such thing, no way to distinguish between those indulgent pleasures and real life. Even more telling, coming home means coming back to a life without her father, an existence that she and her siblings still pine over.

As my daughter looked at me with annoyance, I felt unappreciated. Unwanted. No, I cannot woo her with lavish suites at five-star hotels and extravagant gifts at the drop of a hat. Even if I could, I wouldn't because that's not my way. I believe in living comfortably but within my means, and I don't think the finest things in life automatically equate to a finer quality of life. In fact, I think the opposite.

In the next room, my son, who vomited on the plane after having had too little sleep and inner ear issues from the cabin pressure, lay in bed trying to stave off nausea and fight a bad headache. He was already worried he would be unable to attend the baseball game and spend the last night of spring break with his father.

When my ex arrived at four-thirty to pick up the children for the seven o'clock game, a nice dinner reservation awaiting them at the stadium beforehand, my son still felt too sick to leave. My ex offered to stay behind, skipping the game in lieu of a pizza and movie night, but my daughters really wanted to go. I could tell my ex was torn, and I felt for him. In a gallant maneuver, my son, not wanting to ruin everyone else's good time, sent them on their way. After the door closed, he started to cry, so I promised him that if he felt better in an hour, I would drive him to the stadium in time for the first pitch. Exactly one hour later, after the Advil kicked in, my son came downstairs ready to leave.

In rush hour traffic, I began making my way from my northern New Jersey home to Queens and, despite my normally accurate navigation system, still managed to get lost along the way. The trip took longer than it should have, and my ex and I argued on the drive there as he criticized the route I chose.

When I reminded him that this wasn't an insignificant under-taking on my part, he reminded me I was doing this for my son. Of course I was, and I was happy to do it (that's why I offered), but I was also doing this for him, which he refused to acknowledge.

Arriving a little after the game began, I spotted my ex standing outside the stadium at a distance. He waved for my son to get out of the car, not addressing me in the slightest. When my son jumped out and ran to his dad, I suddenly felt like one of those discarded end pieces of bread back in my freezer; the piece everyone handles but no one wants to keep.

As I turned my car around to head home in even more traffic, I thought about my role as a divorced single mom. In many respects, I'm like those end pieces of bread. My husband left me, passed me by for what he seems to believe is a better, more appetizing piece. Out in the dating world, I feel like those end slices when a man wants to date me, but the relationship fails to grow into one I would like, in part because of my cir-cumstances. So yes, if I see myself in these terms, I'm one of those forsaken ends.

When I arrived home three hours after I left, I braced my-self for the night to come, one filled with overtired children and harrowing goodbyes. True to form, the night played out as an-ticipated, and there I was, again, comforting my children as they assimilated back into their world.

Once I got the kids to bed, I thought about it. I'm similar to the heels of a bread loaf all right, but in a good way. Those end slices of bread play a crucial role. They protect the softer pieces of bread, the slices more vulnerable to damage. Those end pieces are strong. They have a thick crust and can withstand

191

more than their soft counterparts. They stand steadfast and tall, hugging either side of the bread loaf, holding it together with their backs to the wind.

Those who have been divorced—those who struggle to keep their family united, balanced, and safe—know how weighty it can feel to be an end piece of bread. Caring for and protecting a whole loaf is a big responsibility, and the job may sometimes make us feel lonely, unappreciated, and exposed. But the truth is those ends serve a vital purpose, and the reward for having such a position can be most gratifying. So today, with my new loaf of forgotten ends, I'm going to a bake bread pudding, knowing full well it's those stale, crusted ends that help hold our families and our lives together.

The Rainbow Connection: How I Know We're Not Alone

I don't believe there are any accidents. Yet most would argue I was involved in two this past Saturday night.

It started like any ordinary day. I had raced around since early that morning in anticipation of spending a quiet evening in the city with my boyfriend at the time. My week had been a trying one—arguing with the ex, a sick child, and even a broken oven to boot, all coming on top of the usual craziness. But it was as I prepared to leave my house that I received the worst news of the previous few days—that my stepfather had gotten sick and was rushed by ambulance to the hospital. I would spend the next few hours waiting for word of his condition until finally hearing from my mother later that night he was OK.

As I made my way to Manhattan through a torrential downpour, I thought back on the week's comings and goings and wondered why my life must always be so difficult. I am, by most accounts, a nice person; considerate, helpful whenever I can be, and empathetic. Yet time and time again, I feel as though I simply cannot catch a break. In truth, I know this isn't the case. I'm well aware it's only the way I'm looking at things at the present moment that makes me think this way. But we all have our bad days. This happened to be one of them.

Less than fifteen minutes from my destination, I stopped at a traffic light. Looking up at the sky, I saw the most beautiful rainbow high above the rooftops. "It's a sign," I thought. Seeing a rainbow in most cultures is a good omen, so I assured myself I must have some much-needed luck coming my way.

And then I made a wrong left turn. I was supposed to turn two hundred and fifty feet up ahead but jumped the gun. Now I would either have to go around the block or head uptown on the traffic-filled avenue I had originally tried to avoid. As I kicked myself, a truck got too close and knocked off the driver's side mirror on my car.

"Unbelievable!" I grumbled. "So much for rainbows."

One police report and the other driver's arrest for driving with a suspended license later, I was back on my way, managing to take the most recent events in stride.

After four hours and a fun evening, I began my trek back to New Jersey. Suddenly, BOOM! The noise was loud but unidentifiable. As I would soon discover, I had hit a monstrous-sized pothole in the center of the road.

My car immediately began to drag, then ceased seconds later right there in the middle of the on-ramp to a city highway. With no power at all, I couldn't even put my hazard lights on. I dialed 911, but as I watched cars, trucks, and city buses maneuver around me, I recognized the perilous situation in which I now found myself.

New Yorkers get a bad rap for being self-involved and unhelpful. I disagree. Within seconds, a car pulled up behind me to assist. Two men jumped out. Not having any success starting the car either, they waited for the police to come, their hazard lights on to protect me from being hit by another vehicle.

When the men had to go, another couple of good Samaritans pulled over. They, too, tried to move my car off to the side of the road. Unsuccessful, they spotted cones sitting at the curb nearby and placed them behind my car. When a squad car and tow truck arrived soon after, I believed I was out of harm's way.

I wasn't.

As it turned out, I could only be towed into the city because of some weird contractual restriction. So the tow truck driver left me with my disabled car one block from where I had broken down to wait for a second tow truck to take the car and me back to New Jersey. That was the plan. The events that unfolded over the next seven hours would reveal a far different one.

There I sat, in my car, windows unable to close and car doors unable to lock, in a quiet residential neighborhood with a city park off to my right. Though the calendar said it was spring, Mother Nature hadn't gotten the message. Once the sun went down, it felt like winter.

When the second tow truck arrived within the hour, the driver couldn't put the car in neutral, which was, so I was told, necessary for towing. After many repeated attempts, the driver advised I would need yet another tow truck, one outfitted with different towing equipment. He offered to let me wait with him in his warm truck until either AAA or OnStar could send additional help.

When help did finally arrive—a third tow truck driver, this one a "repo" guy—my hopes were high. If anyone could get my car moving, it would be this guy. But he couldn't start the car either. His truck also didn't have the right equipment for towing a car not in neutral, so he left. The second tow truck driver stayed.

But when he received a road call, I had to go back to my cold car to wait. Though he promised to return, I was skeptical. After all, he had no reason to. As I sat by myself, the hours dragging on and the temperature outside growing colder, the streets became deserted. Both AAA and OnStar stayed in contact with me, reassuring me of their efforts, but they were still not having any luck finding the truck I needed at that hour of the night.

Alone in my cold car next to a dark park in the middle of the night, unable to lock myself in, I felt like a sitting duck. I tried not to imagine what else could possibly go wrong, but I would be lying if I said I wasn't afraid. I did my best, but the tears finally did come.

Then out of nowhere and without a word to me, two NYPD squad cars pulled up—one parking alongside me, one in front—and waited. The tow truck driver did eventually return, and the police left. For the next few hours, I sat with this man in his truck as efforts were made to find help. Leaving my car wasn't an option, as the city would impound it, and I would be in the same predicament come Monday.

Finally, around 4:30 in the morning, I received word that a tow truck from New Jersey was on its way. And just as quickly as my hopes were raised, they were dashed by a follow-up call informing me the truck wasn't coming because a call from the police took priority over mine. At this point, I had hit the pothole nearly five hours earlier, yet I was still no closer to getting home.

Not long after, another call came in. A truck would be arriving within the next twenty minutes, and I could be confident this driver had the equipment I needed. I had little faith. But when he did arrive, the fourth tow truck driver that night, towing the car appeared effortless. We were finally on our way. It was now 5:00 a.m. He stopped at a restaurant so I could use the bathroom, and I accompanied him on a quick service call he had delayed for mine.

As I watched the sun come up in the city early Sunday morning, I was exhausted and shaken, but more than anything, confused as to why I had been unfortunate enough to have gone through this rattling experience. I chatted with the driver, an immigrant from India, and discovered he, too, was divorced; he and his ex-wife and children now living apart because they failed to agree on which city to call home.

His story was eerily similar to my own, making me wonder if this night was somehow meant to be. He sounded like my ex-husband as he told me his wife chose the comfort of remaining close to her extended family down south rather than moving back with him to New York. My ex argues I chose the comfort of my New Jersey home rather than relocating to Hong Kong, where his career directed him and where he wanted to live. This man, retelling his side of his marriage's demise, recounted a version I'm sure ran contrary to that of his ex-wife. But as I know well, there are two sides to every story, and then there's the truth. It's only a matter of what we choose to see.

Making my way back home, I realized I wasn't unlucky that night but, rather, extremely fortunate. Yes, a lot had gone wrong. But throughout the night, there was almost always someone there to help and guide me, and I remained safe.

Since my separation, and at times during my marriage, I've felt isolated and alone. I often think there's no way I will have the strength to make it one more day by myself. Yet I'm reluctant to accept assistance from people when they offer it, perhaps out of fear they won't be there for me when I do really need them. I'm afraid to let my guard down because I think, often to my detriment, it's better to be alone than disappointed. And probably my most misguided thought: I believe taking help from others is somehow a show of weakness.

I've been wrong.

So many people stepped forward for me, from the beginning of the night until the wee hours of the morning. From offers of comfort and support to protection from the cold and harm's way to emergency childcare, I received a life-affirming message that I'm not alone.

We're not alone.

As for that rainbow? Upon further reflection, I must say seeing it was by far the best luck I've had in a long, long time.

For Whom the Wedding Bells Toll

When my eldest daughter was three (she's almost fifteen now), she decided to throw our family cat a first birthday party. She crafted noisemakers and party hats from construction paper for everyone in our immediate family, including the cat. My girls and I baked a homemade cake (for us) and decorated it. And after dinner on the night of his party, we all sat around the table singing "Happy Birthday" to our furry family member. The party was so precious it became a family tradition, and we have celebrated the cat's birthday this way ever since.

As the years passed, either my husband or myself would snap a quick picture of the kids at the party. The photo would be the same each time, with little variation; one of our three children holding the cat on their lap, while the other two kids huddled closely around one another, grinning wide, toothy smiles over a birthday cake with a burning numerical candle and one extra for good luck.

"Make a wish," I never failed to instruct the cat (wink, wink) just before taking his picture. My kids laughed every single time because I sounded so ridiculous. But silently, I always made his wish for him.

In January of 2012, my husband and I separated. We briefly reconciled over Passover three months later, but after realizing that being married was something neither of us wanted, we officially separated on April 8, also the cat's birthday.

Our divorce was imminent, and my husband left for Hong Kong that afternoon. As our family tradition dictated, the children and I celebrated the cat's birthday after dinner, this time without my husband. The party was bittersweet, familiar yet lonely. But we pressed on anyway, even though none of us felt like celebrating.

That was three years ago.

Before my children left last week to spend spring break with their dad, they reminded me the day they were scheduled to return would be the cat's birthday, his thirteenth, and requested I buy a cake so we could celebrate. However, in my confusion, I forgot. When the children found out, my eldest daughter asked her dad to buy a cake before going to the airport. He agreed, and the two of them left to get one.

That's when my ten-year-old son told me: "Daddy got married last week."

I looked up from my computer screen, dumbfounded.

"Are you sure?" I asked, knowing a large wedding celebration was penned on the calendar for late August and knowing even better my son was waiting for my response to gauge his own.

"Yes," my younger daughter confirmed. "He told us the day before yesterday. We asked if you already knew, but Dad said it was none of your business. He wanted us to tell you after he went home."

But before I could fully comprehend the news, in walked my ex-husband and daughter, birthday cake in hand.

"I hear congratulations are in order," I asked, prodding him.

200

"For what?" he said, pretending he didn't have a clue.

"Didn't you get married last week?"

My ex-husband looked down at the floor. "Yes," he answered, emotionless. "I did."

I hesitated before speaking, my atypical silence eventually forcing him to look at me as he braced for my response, the way a misbehaved child awaits his punishment.

But that evening, there would be no tongue lashing. Not from me.

"You're a lucky guy," was my one and only remark.

With that, I picked up the cake from the kitchen counter and brought it to the table, where we all sang "Happy Birthday" in unison.

Before blowing out the candles, our children posed for their annual picture as they always did, a moment I doubted my ex-husband and I would ever share again.

For the longest time, I anticipated how I would feel on his wedding day, the day he would marry someone else, that someone being the woman who facilitated and expedited the end of our marriage. Would I be sad? Would I be happy? Would I feel anything at all?

I no longer have to wonder. That day came and went without my even knowing, truly a blessing in disguise.

My ex-husband and I spent twenty-four years together, sixteen of them married. We've known each other since we were teens and share three children. Yet he thought nothing about keeping his nuptials from me, instructing our children to do the same.

At first, I was offended. Hurt. Angry. But not because he married someone else. No, that wasn't it at all. It was because I believed I was deserving of something more from him, that something being respect.

Indignant as I initially was, the truth is he's no longer my husband. And what he owes me, apart from his legal obligations as per our divorce agreement, is absolutely nothing. A friend took the liberty of explaining this to me. Yes, he could have done things differently. Been more considerate of my feelings. But he didn't. And he wasn't. Truth be told, there's not a damn thing I can do about it.

With or without his respect, what I do believe is life has a way of turning out for the best, even when it may not always seem possible. The end of our marriage was one of those instances. Though the children were disappointed with the latest news, they are each doing fine.

"Make a wish," I teased the cat, just like I had done during all those previous birthday parties.

As our children blew out the cat's candles with ease and a lightheartedness I once worried I would never see again, I wished that my home, the one we worked so hard to rebuild over these past three years, would continue to be the happy home it has finally come to be.

So yes, my ex-husband is a lucky guy. Very lucky indeed. We all are.

And Baby Makes . . . How Many?

In the past, I would've driven to a Walgreens in a town far, far away. I've done it before. Not often, but at least once since becoming separated a little more than three years ago. Honestly, I don't care who I run into at this point in my life. So you see my forty-two-year-old ass standing in line at the register holding a pregnancy test. So what? If you do, at least you will likely assume I've been having some fun. And that's more than I can say about a lot of people I know, maybe even yourself. Hell, once upon a time, I could've easily said it about me.

No more.

True to my word, about a month ago, when I realized my period was overdue (not a frequent occurrence), I yelled to my three kids doing homework upstairs that I was running a quick errand and headed toward my very local Walgreens. Bring it on. I was prepared to meet anybody—my rabbi, best friend, even the school secretary. Anyone. Of course, being that I was prepared for that chance encounter, I didn't have one. It was only me, myself, and I standing in aisle three among a myriad of pregnancy tests.

I must say, even to this day, buying a pregnancy test is an exhilarating experience. It's exciting to think about the prospect of creating another life with someone I love, respect, and admire. That would not be the case this time, but, in theory, a new baby is always nice to imagine, even for a moment.

In fact, I did always want another baby, a sentiment also shared by my children. And I went so far as to tell my husband I was finally ready to have our fourth child, the one we talked about often up until a couple of weeks before our marriage ended. By that point, he was no longer interested, though I had yet to learn the specific reason why.

Back at home, while I waited for a second pink line to appear, I was reminded of those other times I saw it and how happy I was. This time, there would be no second line (in reality, a good thing), and I headed to my OB-GYN later that week, where she confirmed I wasn't pregnant and chalked up my lack of punctuality to stress. It makes perfect sense, of course. Stress is the reason I'm late for everything else these days, so why make an exception here?

And late I was. To the party, that is. In actuality, I wasn't even invited. Not invited to last Saturday night's wedding (my ex's niece's) or the rehearsal dinner on the night preceding it where my ex told our children during the cocktail hour his new wife was ten weeks pregnant.

Though the announcement came as little surprise to my two daughters and me (despite my ex's ardent protests to the contrary only hours earlier), my ten-year-old, who particularly struggles with his father's absence, took the news badly. Upon hearing, he pulled out his cell phone to call me but was strongly advised by his father not to. Thankfully, my daughters noticed their little brother standing alone crying and comforted him.

So often when we speak of divorce, we speak of it in terms of starting a new life for ourselves. But what we don't always take into consideration is how hard it can be to watch those around us start a new life for themselves as well. And this can be just as much if not more difficult than the former.

A new baby no longer appears to be in the cards for me, and that's OK. I love my three children to pieces, and I'm so grateful they're mine. I also know I may become a stepmother one day, and I look forward to and welcome such an opportunity. But that doesn't mean watching my ex start a new family with someone else is at all comfortable. Even worse is watching my children feel cheated because of it.

On the bright side, my children are finally going to get that little sibling they always wanted, despite the baby being born from the stepmom they do not love instead of the mom they do. But they love their dad too. And that has to be enough—for now.

I do anticipate how difficult it may be for my three children to watch their dad live in the same home with his new child when he has chosen to live so far from them. There's no getting around it. But I will be supportive because that's what life after divorce is all about—dealing with the fallout and being able to glean the good from those situations that do not always make us feel so good, at least not at first.

When my ex shared his good news with our children, he told them how fortunate they are to soon have one more person in the world to love them. About that, he's absolutely correct. We can all benefit from more love.

And since the best way to get love is first to give it, my children are destined for plenty.

When the 'Family' Pet Dies after Divorce: How I Said Goodbye

I never had a pet growing up. Not even a goldfish. So when my then-husband suggested I adopt an ASPCA kitten from a work event I was attending while he was toiling away at the office late one night back in 1999, I agreed. After filling out the required paperwork, I was on my way home with our first "baby."

And baby he was, especially as his love and companionship helped bring me back from the depression I experienced after miscarrying my first pregnancy.

When I did eventually become a mother for the first time a little over a year later, the cat was already an integral part of our family.

He died unexpectedly at the age of three while I was pregnant with my second daughter, and I vowed never again to own another pet. Losing an animal, especially one I loved so much and who was so closely associated with trauma in my life, was something I never wanted to experience again.

My husband, a long-time animal lover, had other ideas.

It was on a weekend visit to a pet store with our baby girls strapped wide-eyed into their double stroller, unwitting accessories to what was about to happen, that a store clerk directed us to a cage housing a Ragdoll kitten inside.

The store clerk handed the kitten to my husband, who introduced the frightened animal to our young girls.

"Would you like to hold him?" my husband asked me.

"No," I replied, maintaining my distance.

"Just hold him," my husband urged, placing the kitten into my arms.

When I did, that tiny kitten looked straight at me. Right then, I knew he was ours.

Almost two weeks ago, more than thirteen years later, I found myself driving that same little guy, our Louie, from one hospital to another, the second of which would be better equipped to offer him the emergency care he needed.

For the duration of the forty-minute drive, he lay next to me in my eldest daughter's arms, wrapped in a blanket. Midway through the trip, I caught him arching his head back toward me out of the corner of my eye.

"What is he doing?" I asked my daughter as I continued to focus on the road.

"He's trying to see you, Mommy," she answered.

I glanced over and met his upside-down stare. The look we exchanged was the same as on the day we first met.

Forty-eight hours later, he was gone.

We're each grieving in our own way over the loss of our beloved pet, family member, friend, and confidant.

But, for me, there's something more—the loss of yet another connection to life before my divorce.

Louie grew up with our family. When he was young, he traveled to Hong Kong and lived with us there for three years.

He was part of the welcoming committee along with my daughters when my husband and I brought our son home from the hospital.

For years, Louie remained my three children's playmate, suffering through countless costume changes and photo shoots, as well as endless and not always so gentle hugs and kisses. He was a good sport throughout, and my guess is he loved (almost) every minute of it.

Louie grew up with me as I began my new life as a divorced single parent, never letting me sleep alone, not once, while my kids were away with their dad or allowing me to sit by myself on the couch watching TV. He helped fill what I at one time believed was an unfillable void in my life.

When Louie got sick, I was willing to go to extreme measures (and expense) to save him. My ex-husband, not so much. It was clear he had long since moved on—from me, from Louie, from our life together—and advised I put the cat down without a fight.

I didn't listen.

As Louie fought to come home, first surviving a risky procedure only to face new complications afterward, emotions ran high. So, too, did the hospital bill.

The doctors made us choose: rigorous treatment or euthanasia.

We made the decision as a family. Secretly, I hoped the children would be the excuse I needed to prolong his life. They weren't. They were the rational ones, refusing to let Louie suffer any longer than he needed to.

The loss of Louie, as devastating as it is, is a gentle reminder that there eventually comes the point when we must let go of our past. As I've learned over the last few years, letting go comes piecemeal and doesn't necessarily become any easier even with the passage of time.

In the days following Louie's death, I suggested to my children that we welcome another cat into our lives one day. They responded the same way I had so many years ago, telling me they didn't want another pet.

Having loved Louie for more than thirteen years, today I know better.

Quietly, I've begun the search.

If, as I suspect, I'm met with resistance down the road, I know exactly what I'll say: "Just hold him."

The Day a Wasp Invaded My Nest

The other day my eldest daughter had a wasp in her room. And I'm not talking about the country club type.

Yeah, yeah, I know. She's a teenager and pushing fifteen, and I really shouldn't joke about such matters. After all, I met the guy (not a WASP) who would one day become my ex-husband when I was just around her age.

As romantic as it sounds, I have to tell you I would've preferred some blonde-haired, blue-eyed, ruddy-cheeked future yachtsman all decked out in Vineyard Vines to what I was met with behind my daughter's closed door. Because, let me say, the scene was disturbing. Mostly to me, even though my daughter was the one screeching like someone about to get axed in a horror movie.

And I blame marriage. Not only mine but the institution in general.

Sounds harsh, right? And ridiculous. I know. I understand what you're thinking—another bitter rant from some woman who believes all bad luck stems from her divorce.

Not true. Not true at all. But please, let me explain.

For starters, I hadn't gone to the bathroom in hours. So naturally, that's when all of this went down. But since my kids aren't toddlers anymore and haven't been for years, I thought I could go five minutes without (a) Jamie Lee Curtis-type screams emanating from one of my children the moment I was out of sight, and (b) one of my children banging on the bathroom door while I was inside.

I must have been deluded.

Because whenever it comes to indulging in a little "me" time, even if it's in the form of doing my business (not quite the luxury I've always dreamed of but, hey, I take what I can get), I'm summoned for tasks I would never have imagined doing all those years ago as I walked through Neiman's picking out china for my bridal registry. Cleaning cat vomit, kid vomit, plunging toilets . . . You get the idea.

I learned early on it was all part of the job description. That is except for this one little thing I simply refused to take on.

Throughout my marriage, despite my being quite the independent stay-at-home wife and mom, there were still tasks I continued to deem the man's job. Killing bugs was at the top of that list. Exterminator was a title my husband begrudged (and I mean just short of kicking and screaming in protest), holding it for more than sixteen years until he quit.

My divorce has since charged me with this duty, and I believe I've not only taken over the job but also run with it. Except when that insect has a stinger.

Then I just run.

Which is what I did long ago after experiencing my first sting. My friend's dad swatted a bee off my back with a towel, and it stung me.

At only three years old, I can remember like it was yesterday; her mom driving me home from their country club in her blue station wagon, me in hysterics in the front seat (and, in those days, without a seat belt), and my friend trying, without success, to console me.

My fear of bees and other stinging insects lived on through my adolescence and into my adulthood. To this day, I scream at every buzz within earshot. (Reason #403 why I'm no longer married.) Then I got separated. No longer could I afford to be afraid. But I was. I just hid it better now that my kids were watching.

Believe me when I tell you that any insect in my midst paid a hefty price for my fear, enjoying a slow and painful death by suffocation as I confined each one to an overturned drinking glass. Either my cleaning lady would dispose of the body on her weekly Monday visit or, if it met its untimely death (untimely for the insect but not timely enough for me) sooner, I would suck it up with my vacuum cleaner.

I managed to get through more than five years on my own without incident. And I was damn proud of myself.

Then four days ago, all of that changed.

Enter Jamie Lee Curtis scream.

And the biggest, baddest wasp I had ever seen. My daughter actually snapped a picture of it a day earlier as it hung out outside her window screen while noshing on a bright green creepy crawler. I most definitely would've deemed it vacuum-worthy had it been inside.

Now that it was inside, I wondered if I should call an exterminator. A neighbor, perhaps? Animal control? None of those options felt right. So after rummaging around for bug spray and not finding any, I headed out to buy a can.

As I drove home from the store, I remained remarkably calm. Chill. I had this down. No fear.

Until I was standing outside the door with the spray, ready to attack.

One adult. One kid.

Guess who headed in first. And not at all.

Embarrassing, I know. Granted, she had on a makeshift beekeeper's uniform she put together herself. Then there was me, who stood at the door an arm's length away, Raid in hand.

My daughter spotted the wasp resting comfortably on a picture frame on her dresser. I pummeled it quickly from a safe distance away. It fell backward, landing somewhere behind the furniture. However, when she went to look for it after, it wasn't there.

That was Wednesday. Still wearing the homemade beekeeper's uniform, my daughter proceeded to move everything she needed out of her bedroom and into mine, where she bunked until Sunday morning when she and her sister left for a month-long teen tour. My son left for sleepaway camp a day earlier, which means I'm now officially alone, with the wasp, who has yet to make an encore appearance.

Until this morning, towels lined the bottom of my daughter's door so the new tenant inside couldn't escape. But when my cleaning lady arrived, she searched high and low and found nothing either. Hearing the news, I reluctantly took the towels away, knowing full well that if I saw the wasp again, no one was going to come running.

I thought about how I spent many years married to a workaholic husband who was rarely home. Out of sheer necessity, I became as independent as anyone coupled could.

Or so I thought.

In actuality, I still relied on my marriage, on my husband specifically, for protection. At the end of the day, I depended on him to take care of me and make everything better when I couldn't.

No one should ever have to live up to that standard.

When my husband walked out, I lost his protection. And I was, for the first time in my life, on my own.

It was scary. Petrifying, actually.

But as I slowly recoup the independence I once willingly abdicated to him—by earning my own money, by taking full responsibility for how I feel, and by overcoming my fears—I see how marriage is about something other than being taken care of by your spouse.

Marriage is about continuing to grow as an individual with your complement by your side. It's about growing stronger, not weaker, in another person's company. If your marriage becomes something else, it's time for a change.

No one should be doing things for you that you can do for yourself to the point where you never learn how to do them. Ever.

So often I come across married women who claim they're incapable of making small household repairs, putting air in their tires, or finding a way to earn their own money. They believe they need their husbands to survive. I, too, was guilty of this.

My days of needing my ex-husband—for anything—are now numbered, which makes me happy. And proud.

Married or not, I must remember to take care of myself first. Be there for my partner, whoever he may be, as his added support, not his only support. And allow my partner to be there for me by letting him only do what I can continue to do for myself in his absence.

That wasp is still lurking somewhere inside my house, which means I must face another one of my fears today. But the good news is, when I do, I know I will be less afraid of tomorrow.

How Can You Act This Way After So Many Bad Things Have Happened to You?

December 31, 2015

When my husband left just days after the new year in January of 2012, we had already planned a family vacation to Cabo San Lucas for that coming April.

Not comfortable traveling on my own to Mexico with three little ones in tow (at the time, they were eleven, ten, and seven), I canceled that trip and booked another at an all-inclusive family resort in Turks and Caicos for the sake of simplicity. My mother and stepfather joined us at the last minute for moral support.

Amid blue skies, topaz water, and white sandy beaches, we (especially me) were anything but smiles, even in such a beautiful setting.

Beginning on day one, I mentally checked out as I lay by the pool with my iPod on full blast, watching my kids play by themselves in the water. Their attention span was shorter than normal, as was my own during those early days after my separation, and they were fighting with each other nonstop.

It didn't take a genius to understand why. The kids missed their dad and were expressing themselves the only way they knew how.

I did nothing to intervene. I just couldn't.

As the week wore on, so, too, did their irritation. And mine. Adding insult to injury, my son's iTouch was stolen off a restaurant table when he left it behind.

On our second to last day there, my eldest daughter verbalized what we had all been thinking: "This vacation stinks."

She was right.

As I stood in the suite I had paid for with money I should have been saving, my heart ached. I had failed. I had failed at my marriage and, as a result, had failed at parenthood. Defeated, I sat on my bed in the middle of the afternoon and reflected on my own childhood.

For the first part of my life, I was raised in what I now recognize as an abusive home. In between brief periods of mania, my father berated my mother, threw things (sometimes at her), spit on her, slapped her across the face on a few occasions, and poured a glass of grape juice over her head. If we were in the car and he didn't like something my mother said, he would jerk the steering wheel so hard that my brother and I would go flying across the backseat from the force of it, landing on top of one another. He told my mother that if she left him, he would take us away from her.

Then, when I was thirteen, he dropped dead, leaving my mother $26 in his wallet and a mountain of debt. If not for the house my parents owned together, I am afraid to imagine what would have become of us.

I think I can speak for most parents when I say it is our sincerest hope that we give our kids a childhood akin to the one we had (if it was good) or a better one if ours had its rough spots.

Having spent more than twenty-four years with a man who did not respect me, today claims he never loved me, displayed (and continues to display) affection almost entirely through gift-giving, and who thought nothing of making his life 8,000 miles from our three children, I should have known better than to think a week away would be the quick fix I was looking for.

I do not recall many happy memories from my childhood. But the few I do include those moments when my father would grab my mother, her apron still tied tightly around her waist, and dance to their old records from the '60s that I played over and over again while my mother cooked dinner.

I would scramble to a corner in our family room and look up at them, sitting on the floor with my legs crisscrossed as they danced to the songs of Dion, The Supremes, and The Byrds. The expression on their faces harkened to another time—a happier one—and served as a beacon of hope that someday life would again be calm.

Emerging from my reverie back in our island hotel room, I reached for the iPod that had carried me away all week and placed it in the docking station on my nightstand. With the same music from my past, I coaxed my children from their beds. Within minutes, my kids and I were dancing, laughing, and singing without a care in the world about how we looked or sounded.

As it has during my entire life, music has followed me through the last four years since my marriage ended, guiding me over hurdles and around obstacles I have encountered, including the most recent.

Earlier this month, my ex-husband became a father for the fourth time with his once mistress and now second wife, making what was at first a painful possibility a new reality for us all.

I was away for the weekend when my children first received the news and, to my surprise, was more detached than I anticipated I would be. My kids, on the other hand, felt sad and conflicted as their father described with excitement the new baby that he would be raising an ocean away as he spoke to them over FaceTime.

While preparing dinner later that week for my family—as my mother had done so many years ago for my younger brother and me—my son, now ten, sat at our kitchen counter playing music from his iPod. As we sang along to Ariana Grande and Justin Bieber, my two other children walked in, the older of whom stared at me wide-eyed.

"What?" I asked her as I danced around the room, gesticulating to the music for added effect.

"How can you act this way after so many bad things have happened to you?" she replied.

I stopped to catch my breath. It was a question I had never before considered but a question to which I now know I always had the answer.

"Because," I told her, "there is 'a time to mourn, and a time to dance'" (Eccl. 3:4 KJV).

Which brings me to today, the third New Year's Eve since my husband and I finalized our divorce in 2013.

I have spent the past four years mourning the end of my sixteen-year marriage, a relationship that began with a first date on New Year's Eve back in 1987 and ended exactly twenty-four years later with what would become our last on December 31, 2011. Since then, I have commemorated New Year's Eve with my family, using it as a time to reflect and focus on what I have lost instead of what I have gained.

In keeping with this mentality, for the past two years, I have written about my longing for a New Year's Eve kiss, something I have missed since separating. This year, I will not be making such a pronouncement. There will be no sorrowful blog post written that night nor any self-defeating rituals in which I will partake. And not because I have someone to kiss me this New Year's Eve.

I do not.

But what I do know is this: wherever I am and whoever I am with, even if it is no one at all, what I will do is dance. Because "[t]o every thing there is a season" (Eccl. 3:1 KJV), and that season is now.

Epilogue

In the days after my husband announced he was "done with our marriage," I began reaching out to family members (his and mine) as well as our friends for help. The help was not for me, though. It was at the time for my husband and what I believed, naively, he needed. In my mind, he was going through a phase and would snap out of it as one typically does when in a bad mood. I requested they talk some sense into my husband and convince him he had made and was making another grievous mistake: first by engaging in an extramarital affair with a younger woman and second by leaving me for her.

Some attempted to change his mind; others fueled the fire, not fully comprehending the seriousness of the situation—that my husband's choice meant he would call Hong Kong home, 8,000 miles away from me and, worse still, our young children. Nobody, it seemed, realized it could "go that far," which it did, inevitably turning me into a custodial and single parent.

My efforts were futile. Nothing anyone said to my husband, including me, could change his mind. I realize now I wouldn't have wanted it to, not only because I hadn't yet acknowledged to myself our marriage was long over, but also that a change of heart needed to come from him. It never did. Nor did it from me.

But that didn't stop me first from pleading for his love. In fact, I begged for it and, by doing so, told him I was never good enough to receive it in the first place. Perhaps that is because I never believed I was, a sad state having less to do with him and more with me.

After we split, I set out to find love from others. And thought I found it early on when, in reality, I had only found the familiar, a place where I could feel like I wasn't enough. The truth was, at that point in my life, I wasn't enough. But not because I wasn't pretty enough, smart enough, rich enough, young enough, or successful enough. I was. I just didn't believe it yet. And because I didn't, I accepted bad behavior from men I dated, stayed in bad relationships, and went back to bad relationships, trying to fix the unfixable.

It took years, but eventually, I stopped trying to fix other people. I was frustrated. And tired. With every relationship I began, I felt like I was trying to climb a tree whose branches broke beneath me any time I achieved some height, sending me crashing back to the bottom. So after yet another dating mishap, instead of trying to find the next tree to climb, I stayed in the shade of that tree and regrouped. I revisited my dreams of starting my own business and focused my energies there. I finished the website I had started earlier that year, went live, and officially got to work. It was late 2015.

I found love—in myself. Which made me, for the first time in years, ready to love someone else. The heartbreak I experienced and survived in my marriage and beyond was, although painful, necessary to show me what love is not. Compared to my previous relationships, it is the opposite:

"Love is patient, love is kind. It does not envy, it does not boast, it is not proud. It does not dishonor others, it is not self-seeking, it is not easily angered, it keeps no record of wrongs.

Love does not delight in evil but rejoices with the truth. It always protects, always trusts, always hopes, always perseveres. Love never fails" (1 Cor. 13:4-8 NIV).

Neither do we. We learn. And we grow stronger.

Acknowledgments

There were so many people along the way who made these stories come to life and who made them possible. Then there were those individuals who helped me turn the stories into a book I can now hold in my hands. So that I could comprehend why a particular event took place and, more importantly, remember that I am still here with a louder voice than I ever believed I could have to tell about it. In no particular order because everyone on this list is so important to me, they are:

The readers of my blog from which I spun many of these essays, and the readers who stopped me whenever they saw me, or who wrote to me privately, sometimes anonymously, to say how my words made a difference in their lives.

My many clients, for allowing me to stretch my wings to help them stretch theirs.

Thomas G. Fiffer, for helping me create some semblance of order in such a vast body of work and his role in those early stages of editing.

Unsolicited Press, for sending what I at first thought was a rejection letter. I am so happy I read it to the end. Thank you for taking a chance on me.

My editor, S.R. Stewart, for sending my manuscript back to me, saying, "[t]here's just too much," advising me to cut out almost half, and then encouraging me by saying, "I do believe you have a great book here, but it's buried . . ." Those words have echoed in my mind ever since and are what kept me going throughout this process.

Maddy, Lizzy, and Tyler, my three beautiful, intelligent, talented children, for never failing to tell me what they were thinking and still don't. You are the true loves of my life. Thank you for putting up with me. Those years were not easy, but we made it.

My mother, Janis Brownstein, for listening to me read aloud many of those early essays and making the final call about where a comma should go when I was in doubt. But far more importantly, for the countless nights of babysitting that have come to mean so much. My kids love watching films of every genre because of how many you watched together. They also say Scrabble is their game with you, not to be confused with any game they play with anyone else, including me.

My stepfather, Lennie Brownstein, a.k.a. Grandpa Lennie, for being a great co-babysitter, for talking with the kids about history and politics, and driving Grandma home from my house on all of those late nights.

My brother, Harry Rosenberg, for changing the kitchen calendar after Daddy died.

Mona Pagnozzi, for being that rational ear and then giving it to me straight.

Sydra Miller, for always bringing that unique perspective to the conversation and helping me see a situation in a new light.

Jordana Horn Gordon, for sending me flowers on "Single Mothers Day" all those years ago.

Joanna Huang, for being on this journey with me.

Barbara Brown-Ruttenberg, for going to bat for me whenever I asked for support but, more importantly, those times when I did not ask, and for being on the other end of a six-and-a-half-hour phone call, my longest ever.

The many friends who shared in my adventures. The ones who shall remain nameless to protect the guilty. You know who you are.

The late and great Louie "Luigi" Freeman, for being such a trouper. You are missed.

Bella "Bubsiekins" Freeman, for giving the best hugs and snugs.

David Neff, for his love and support and knack for talking me off the ledge whenever I doubted myself, unparalleled hand-crafted cocktails, especially cosmopolitans and vodka gimlets, and always spot-on sales advice.

Doug Freeman, my ex-husband, whose prescriptions I still pick up at Walgreens all of these years later—by choice—and whose advice I continue to seek every so often and value always. You demonstrated a work ethic I aspired to match, and I believe, have come pretty close. And, of course, for our children who would not be who they are without you.

About the Author

 Stacey Freeman is a writer and journalist and the founder of Write On Track LLC, a full-service consultancy dedicated to providing high-quality content and strategy to individuals and businesses. Her writing has appeared in The Washington Post, The Lily (published by The Washington Post), Forbes, Entrepreneur, MarketWatch, Good Housekeeping, Cosmopolitan, Woman's Day, Town & Country, InStyle, PBS' Next Avenue, AARP, SheKnows, Yahoo!, MSN, HuffPost, POPSUGAR, Your Teen, Grown & Flown, Scary Mommy, CafeMom, MariaShriver.com, and dozens of other well-known platforms worldwide. She lives in New Jersey with her three children.

About the Press

Unsolicited Press was founded in 2012 and is based in Portland, Oregon. The small press publishes fiction, poetry, and creative nonfiction written by award-winning and emerging authors. Some of its authors include John W. Bateman, Anne Leigh Parrish, Adrian Ernesto Cepeda, and Raki Kopernik.

Learn more at www.unsolicitedpress.com

9 781956 692402